New Library of Pastoral Care
GENERAL EDITOR: DEREK BLOWS

Liberating God

New Library of Pastoral Care
GENERAL EDITOR: DEREK BLOWS

—

LIBERATING GOD

Private Care and Public Struggle

—

Peter Selby

First published 1983
SPCK
Holy Trinity Church
Marylebone Road
London NW1 4DU

Publisher's acknowledgement
Excerpts from *Letters and Papers from Prison*
by Dietrich Bonhoeffer (enlarged edition 1971) are reprinted
by permission of SCM Press.

British Library Cataloguing in Publication Data

Selby, Peter
    Liberating God. — (New library of pastoral care)
    1. Pastoral counselling
    I. Title   II. Series
    253.5   BV4012.3

    ISBN 0-281-04066-4

Filmset by Pioneer
Printed.in Great Britain by
the Anchor Press, Tiptree

Contents

Foreword

The *New Library of Pastoral Care* has been planned to meet the needs of those people concerned with pastoral care, whether clergy or lay, who seek to improve their knowledge and skills in this field. Equally, it is hoped that it may prove useful to those secular helpers who may wish to understand the role of the pastor.

Pastoral care in every age has drawn from contemporary secular knowledge to inform its understanding of man and his various needs and of the ways in which these needs might be met. Today it is perhaps the secular helping professions of social work, counselling and psychotherapy, and community development which have particular contributions to make to the pastor in his work. Such knowledge does not stand still, and pastors would have a struggle to keep up with the endless tide of new developments which pour out from these and other disciplines, and to sort out which ideas and practices might be relevant to their particular pastoral needs. Among present-day ideas, for instance, of particular value might be an understanding of the social context of the pastoral task, the dynamics of the helping relationship, the attitudes and skills as well as factual knowledge which might make for effective pastoral intervention, and perhaps most significant of all, the study of particular cases, whether through verbatim reports of interviews or general case presentation. The discovery of ways of learning from what one is doing is becoming increasingly important.

There is always a danger that a pastor who drinks deeply at the well of a secular discipline may lose his grasp of his own pastoral identity and become 'just another' social worker or counsellor. It in no way detracts from the value of these professions to assert that the role and task of the pastor are quite unique among the helping professions and deserve to be clarified and strengthened rather than weakened. The theological commitment of the pastor and the appropriate use of his role will be a recurrent theme of the series. At the same time the pastor cannot afford to work in a vacuum. He needs to be able to communicate and co-operate with those helpers in other disciplines whose work may overlap, without loss of his own unique role. This in turn will mean being able to communicate with them through some understanding of their concepts and language.

Finally, there is a rich variety of styles and approaches in pastoral work within the various religious traditions. No attempt will be made to secure a uniform approach. The Library will contain the variety, and even perhaps occasional eccentricity, which such a title suggests. Some books will be more specifically theological and others more concerned with particular areas of need or practice. It is hoped that all of them will have a usefulness that will reach right across the boundaries of religious denomination.

DEREK BLOWS
Series Editor

Preface

I welcome Peter Selby's new book on the context of pastoral care. It is a disturbing book. That is, it questions many of the prevailing assumptions of pastoral theory and practice. But it is also a creative book. It has about it that hint of the poetic which provokes us to see things in a different light, so that the picture as a whole acquires a new and strangely compelling power.

It has for a long time been widely assumed that a pastoral ministry is concerned with individuals as individuals, but the author skilfully uncovers the distortions which such an assumption conceals. Individual persons are the persons they are, not only because of what they are in themselves, but also because of the world they inhabit responsively and responsibly. Thus there can be no separation of inward and outward, spiritual and political. This theme in itself is not especially novel, but the way in which it is developed in its present context, by the use of imagery drawn reflectively from experience, affords us an unusually striking sense of the potential wholeness of human life, a wholeness which is aware of incompleteness and partiality and embraces both success and failure, falling and standing upright again.

Not everything that Peter Selby proposes will command immediate assent. For example, the concept of 'solidarity' which he favours seems to me to need a far more critical treatment than he gives it. Again, I have reservations about the way in which he associates the idea of the 'common good' with the middle classes and the political centre. However, his arguments cannot simply be brushed aside, even where one questions them.

The book as a whole combines to a rare degree both insight and reflection.

PETER BAELZ
Dean of Durham
(Formerly Professor of Moral and Pastoral Theology
in the University of Oxford)

April 1983

Acknowledgements

This book is a revision of material presented as the Kellogg Lectures at the Episcopal Divinity School, Cambridge, Massachusetts, USA in May 1982, under the title 'Human Meaning and Superhuman Struggle: Spirituality and Pastoral Care in Political and Theological Perspective'. Without the invitation to me to be resident as a Procter Fellow and to give these lectures, there would have been no book; without the stimulus provided by that community a much less worthwhile book would have emerged. In particular, Ralph Macy co-ordinated the Procter Programme and organized the lectures and the workshop at which they were discussed; Lloyd Patterson was my supervisor throughout the period, and Doris and Harvey Guthrie lent us their home.

I am also grateful to the Bishop of Newcastle for his support, and to him and colleagues in the diocese of Newcastle for making it possible for me to take a period of sabbatical leave at that time.

A number of friends have made comments which greatly assisted the process of revision: David Carrette identified a number of places where clarification was necessary; Cecilia Goodenough and Alec Graham pointed me clearly in the direction of some of the fundamental questions which are raised in the book; Stephen Pattison very generously did both, as well as sharing with me his immensely valuable research in this field; Geoffrey Smith responded to my initial typescript with a spontaneous vitality and trenchant challenge which have been enormously helpful; and John Nicholson wrote what can only be described as an extended commentary and criticism which is a really valuable piece of theological reflection. Pat Gurr patiently transformed a jumble of scribbles and tapes into a typescript. Finally, had SPCK and

Acknowledgements

Derek Blows not encouraged me in the first instance, I am sure I would not have written this at all.

The support of my family was vital as I tried to write of things very close to me. Benjamin, when he discovered that he had a walk-on part (see Chapter 1), took a very special interest. And if the material can be described as having been born from my head, there is no doubt who the father of it is. When Jan and I first met, she questioned the connection between the political and social content of much of my preaching and the personal element in discipleship. The persistence of her questioning as well as all else we have been able to share have brought this book to birth, and I have been immensely grateful for the way in which she has cherished this child of ours as much as she has our others.

PETER SELBY
Newcastle upon Tyne

March 1983

ONE

The Pastoral Covenant

There is a powerful image that has stayed with me ever since it was first given to me. It has been around in my ministry, to question and to encourage me. It has also supported and encouraged me in moments of personal crisis and exploration. It was given to me by my eldest child when he was in the process of learning to walk.

In my mind's eye I can see him now, sitting on the living-room floor and obviously deciding to make the attempt to reach the other end of the room. He would pull himself up on to his unsteady feet, for all his wobbling nevertheless standing straight; and he would set off. His eyes were on whatever it was that had first attracted his attention at the other end of the room, and he had not a glance to spare for the toys and other obstacles that were scattered all over the living-room floor. Sure enough, the inevitable would happen: he would catch his foot on the pull-along Snoopy dog which in other circumstances had given him so much fun, and he would fall, sometimes just landing on the carpet, sometimes banging some part of himself on the toy dog. Howls of pain and frustration would fill the room, and a nearby parent would pick him up, cuddle him for as long as seemed to be necessary, dry his tears and put him down again. Very soon he would be seen looking at the same object at the far end of the room, deciding yet again to get to his feet and continue the journey. He would set off, still walking upright, still not looking to right or left, with eyes only for his objective. Again he would fail to notice an obstacle in his way, this time his teddy bear. Howls, tears, cuddles, as before. The process would repeat itself many times until, in the short term, he did reach the other end of the room and in the long term, I am happy to report, he learned to walk. In the process he had to learn to take seriously the things that might be lying in his way, to be a little less singleminded about reaching his destination and a little more concerned about the simple, yet vital, business of not falling over. The avoidance of danger became an important and necessary part of success.

Yet the original and foolhardy process of simply going to where he wanted to get has stayed with me as an image. The picture is not for me one of gritty determination, a refusal to be put off by adversity, although no doubt it could be represented that way. What I chiefly notice is the straightness of stance when walking and the totality of collapse when falling, the engrossing excitement of success and the consuming sadness of failure. I notice the absence of that slight stoop which comes with a concern to avoid obstacles and which, literally as well as metaphorically, we assume to belong to a responsible adult in day-to-day living. The overwhelmingly important thing, clearly, was walking, not avoiding a fall. As time goes on, we all have to learn that not falling over things is an essential skill if we are going to walk successfully; but that comes later. In the beginning it is enough to dare, to stand erect, to walk, to fall, to cry, to be held, to be lifted up and to walk again.

There is no way back to our childhood, even if we wish there were. Yet this particular picture of childhood is an important one for adults to look at. They need to look at it, because the process of learning and growing up is not just a process of gaining skills. We also lose some. The capacity to move from upright confidence to abject failure has its own appropriate place in our lives. If we lose that skill, we either have to relearn it, often painfully, or we simply do without it. The caution we cultivate may indeed save us from all kinds of disaster, but it also cuts us off from the immediate experience of ecstasy, passion, grief or rage, so that knowing what we are really feeling becomes that much more difficult. The caution has its value: nobody wants to be a passenger in a car driven by someone who is experimenting with the sensation of moving from confident success to total failure; we demand an appropriate carefulness, and a well-developed capacity to avoid obstacles can be reassuring to anxious front-seat passengers.

That is not, however, always what we most require. Suppose it is not a car driver I am looking for, but a parent, or a friend. If those are what I seek, then I do not require caution as much as the capacity and willingness to walk with me and to fall with me; not only to know what it is to need to be held, to weep and to long to be comforted, but also what it is to want to stand erect, to be strong, to deal responsibly with my own life.

Those whose task is any form of personal ministry will need that capacity too. Those who seek a pastor seek skill, wisdom and learning in the faith; but they also hope to find a person who knows from present experience, and not just as a memory, something of the risks, the dangers and fears that confront anyone who is in the process of learning to walk the earth, or maybe explore some new part of it, with passionate enthusiasm. At such times we do indeed seek the experience of the seasoned explorer, the caution of the guide well acquainted with all the obstacles that there are on the way. But we also need our pastor to be deeply aware of both the majesty and the disaster that are integral to the process of exploration itself. The pastor has to judge, of course, what are the things which need to be shared by those who know with those who do not know, in order to make the journey possible, or inviting, or not too overwhelmingly daunting; equally, though, not too much must be shared in advance, or the journey will become unnecessary or simply boring. It is part of a pastor's skill to make those judgements, and also to take responsibility for misjudgements when they occur. But the only pastors who can even see that judgements of this kind have to be made are ones who, like those for whom they are caring, are also learning to walk in some area of life and who therefore know at first hand what it is like at one moment to own the world and at another to be defeated by it.

The same applies when we are looking for someone who might teach us to pray. We need, of course, the serenity and the wisdom of the experienced guide, someone who has entered deeply into the tradition of praying and has read widely among those who have written about it. There is a place for imparting techniques and for teaching about common hazards and obstacles. The further need is for some sense that the guide is still in touch with the emptiness as well as the glory, the doubt as well as the certainty, that characterize any attempt to grow in spiritual understanding.

We desire an inner sense of unity with the divine will, but we experience just as often a feeling of unquenchable rebellion, and we need our guide to be experiencing that too. There is a walking and a falling before God, and our spiritual journey is as much about that experience as it is about pursuing our aspiration towards a steady progress which avoids the worst and most notorious obstacles.

After all, there is at the heart of the universe not only a will, an intelligence, a purpose with which we desire, by prayer, to identify more fully; all those who have entered seriously into the contemplation of God have experienced what the biblical record also bears witness to: the passionate love, the jealous anger and the profound grief which are the divine response to the beauty, the waywardness and the incompleteness of the world. That being so, the encounter with God is unlikely to be, or to be meant to be, a predictable and steady matter. The help and guidance we need in that encounter, therefore, are likely to come best from a person who knows how to share agony and ecstasy as well as how to take the next steps.

If standing and falling are crucial elements in the experience of learning to walk, it is obvious that context and environment are all-important. It is worth learning to walk when there is enough space for movement to be possible and interesting, and where there are no sharp stones or jagged objects. Children are deeply affected in their development by the surroundings they are offered. The development of the capacity to give and to receive care, and to pray, are also profoundly affected by the context in which they have to be done. We know that, for many, the personal and spiritual journey has to be undertaken in conditions where there is no space to move and no safety to fall. Many are hurt not by sharp stones but by harsh judgements upon them. They are injured early on by the verdict that they are inadequate or blameworthy: a verdict given partly in words, partly by the low priority given to their housing, their education, their health or their culture. Such verdicts quickly produce the stoop of deference or fear.

Every aspect of our growth as persons is affected by the environment which is provided for us, or not provided for us, politically or socially. It is of course true that there are exceptional people and groups of people who transcend their circumstances and show achievement far more impressively than those who start with greater advantages; it is also irrelevant. Contexts do affect the possibilities open to us and pastoral care has to concern itself with the individual's environment if it is to have integrity. Those who, on the one hand, admit people by baptism into the inheritance of the Kingdom of God and, on the other hand, consent to the neglect, the deprivation or the persecution of these same people are dealing in a contradiction which only the most elaborate pretence and defence can prevent both perpetrator and victim from noticing.

The private and the public world of each of us are connected like the strands of a rope and we cannot grow or be cared for in isolation from the world around us. That is not to say that the connection between our inner and outer worlds is simple and direct, or that it is always possible to be clear which is to have the priority. It is simplistic and a gross insult to the world's suffering to speak as though poverty and war will be eliminated by means of the progressive conversion of the hearts of individuals; it is also simplistic, and no less insulting, to suggest that personal maturity and inner resourcefulness are dependent on, or follow automatically from, better living conditions. The connection is more complex than that, but it is there nonetheless. We may have to make a judgement at any particular moment whether our best contribution to a situation is to attend to the environment or the inner world of a person; decisions about priorities will always be situational, but the connection between our inner and outer worlds is more profound than any one situation or the priorities it demands.

The connection between inner and outer worlds is grounded, for most of those who acknowledge it, in reflection on their own experience of what it is to be a person in relationship with other people. The compassion that responds to personal need by acts of help to individuals is not different from the compassion that makes a response by seeking to rectify causes of distress by campaigning, by protest or by political action. The instincts that lead people to give medical aid to the victims of disease in the Third World are not different from the instincts which drive people, often the same people, into campaigning against racism. They are pastoral instincts. Those who counsel and support the victims of rape are not motivated by different aspirations from those who campaign to secure for women the right to walk the streets of our cities free from the fear of sexual assault.

Many who begin by being drawn into acts of individual compassion or by assisting others to come to terms with their inner difficulties are brought quite quickly into a concern for the social roots of those difficulties and into action to rectify them. Others begin by being involved in campaigning, then discover the need to cultivate the inner resources necessary to non-violent resistance or to channelling their anger in appropriate directions. The inner and outer struggles may look different, but they are both struggles for the triumph of love over hatred and hope over despair.

The road that leads from concern with the needs of individuals to public action on their behalf has been taken by a number of Christians whose examples stand out in our time. Martin Luther King did not lead a movement for the civil rights of his people on any other ground than pastoral concern. For pastoral concern is precisely that love of people and that passionate perception of the purpose of God for them which shine through in King's speeches and writings. Those Christians who have committed themselves to political causes demonstrate time and again that they are led into those causes by a deep concern for people and by an overriding religious conviction that oppression simply should not be.

This book, however, does not have its origin in my understanding of what other people have revealed. Its roots lie much closer to the heart of my own life. In so far as I have come to have pastoral concern, it is because I can identify throughout my life the experience of receiving pastoral concern when it was needed. More than that, on those specific occasions when more intensive and explicit pastoral help was needed, it was there for me in people who have been a powerful influence in the putting together of this material. As I contemplate that experience, the conviction grows that the offerings of trust, affection and openness which I have received when I needed them have powerfully formed my convictions about what human beings are meant to be in their life together and what truly co-operative living can be like. We are constantly told that competition is an essential spring of human action, that it is the only route to excellence, and that there is no alternative. I know that this is not so, and I know it because I have been pastored.

It is not, however, only those who have been of help to me, whose fellowship I have experienced in putting these words to paper. There is that other collection of people who, in the process of asking me for help, for time, for the opportunity to gain greater personal clarity or to handle their distress, have given me more and taught me more than they could possibly know. Some of them appear in this book, although for obvious reasons it has been important to change both their names and enough of their characteristics to make them unrecognizable. They are not, however, unrecognized by me as the source of an immense amount of learning. Specifically, they too have taught me what it is possible for us to become together, and that a world in which standing erect and falling totally are permitted can be a safe, exhilarating and majestic place for human beings to live in. They have taught me that listening, counselling and caring are profoundly subversive of entrenched attitudes and oppressive behaviour both in them and in me; they have shown me that the challenge to co-operate is deeply embedded in our most intimate relationships, and that these relationships have the capacity to radicalize us in relation to our understanding of society at large. Where two or three are pastorally gathered together, it is possible to model a new world and in the process to empower the two or three to pursue the overarching aims of justice and peace with greater strength and conviction. Caring is a liberating, socialist activity.

In the process, those who have given me care and received it from me have done much more besides. Not only have individuals been, in some sense, liberated. So also have the great themes and doctrines of Christian faith. They too have been set free to speak with power over a vastly wider area of human life. To watch myself or another move from falling to standing and know that it is safe to fall again is to watch in microcosm the enactment of God's irrevocable covenant with humankind, a covenant which secures the world so that falling and standing are both possibilities for responsible human beings. It is not too much to say that the trusting vulnerability which pastoral care makes possible is a powerful image of the way in which the divine faithfulness awakens the human response of faith. In depicting that faithfulness and that faith, the trusting vulnerability of the pastoral relationship also makes clear that such faithfulness and faith are, to an undreamt-of degree, realizable in the relations of human beings with one another. It is not just that I am meant to respond to faithfulness with faith; *we* as a society are meant to as well. However distant such a world may seem as a prospect, such vulnerability is realizable in the common life of humankind and provides a sounder basis for our life together than the instruments of coercion and domination. Pastoral security is the model of human security.

In pastoral encounter it has also become clear to me that life has a wholeness to it which the New Testament records witness to but which the Church's ways of proclaiming it very often conceal. There are deeply interwoven strands in our lives. The paralysed man is told he is forgiven; he is told he is healed; he is told to walk. *'Absolvo te'*, 'I set you free', is an experience of what is offered to humankind by God; it is realizable in and through the pastoral ministry, but in the process the range of its meaning is widened beyond all expectation. We may come with a problem from which we desire to be set free, and that problem may be intimate and personal, one we hardly dare to confide to anyone. In the process of finding our freedom we are introduced to aspects of our own life and then to aspects of the life of the world where that freedom is also required and offered.

This book is born out of the radicalizing experience of pastoral care. It is written in the conviction that the aims of pastors can be too modest if they are unaware of the power of their pastoral relationships to introduce them to a profounder understanding of the public ills of the world as well as to the great themes of Christian faith.

To be introduced to the connections between private and public, intimate and universal, is to make pastoral decisions much more difficult. It is to bring into our caring a whole range of new issues which we would often sooner forget. As I shall be pointing out, to forget them is not only to diminish the possibilities of pastoral care but also to connive at the continuance of some of the most baleful influences in our public life. It is also to participate in making Christian faith ever more marginal to the major issues of our lives; we make it marginal, not as Jesus was made marginal on a cross, but in the sense that as we seek to preserve our faith inviolate against the challenges of life, so we render it irrelevant to them.

TWO

A Revival of Spirituality?

Spirituality is arousing more interest, or so it seems. As we look around us, do we not gain the unmistakable impression that people are praying again? My evidence here is not statistical; we do not have to become like those who, like guards in some beleaguered ecclesiastical bunker, hail an upward move of a percentage point in confirmation or ordination figures as a major reverse from the powers of darkness. The greater interest in spirituality is.to be seen in both narrower and wider terms than the ecclesiastical statisticians would be able to measure. That greater interest represents a change in the interests of many sensitive people, a discernible shift in their hopes and in the means which they expect to employ in order to discover fulfilment.

In the process 'spirituality' has come to mean a whole range of different activities and concerns. There used to be a clear understanding that spirituality had to do with a rule of life, with daily offices, with meditation exercises and with insights gained from the saints and mystical writers. Now this one word has been claimed by many who wish to speak about and cultivate their inner experience without necessarily having a relationship with any particular tradition of prayer. There is much more talk of 'inner journeys' and 'spiritual well-being' and care is needed to establish what is being referred to by anyone who speaks of these things. It seems that where popularity grows, clarity suffers. Yet, however we evaluate the growing concern with spirituality, it is impossible to write about it without taking into account the broadening of its meaning.

Kenneth Leech, who is as well known for his writings on Christian social and political matters as he is for his concern with spiritual direction, surveys the current growth in interest in spirituality in *Soul Friend*. He had previously, in *Youth-quake,* examined young people's quest for transcendental experience, often undertaken with the aid of drugs. In *Soul Friend* he records the rise of a range of other phenomena all of which form part of the climate as he now sees it. So the increased interest in yoga and transcendental meditation, the Divine Light Mission and the Jesus movement are all instanced. So also are the movements seeking to relate Christian faith to the experience of liberation, and the movement of charismatic renewal. There is an increased awareness, among church members, of the possibilities of contemplative prayer and of the resources of the spiritual tradition in Christianity. We seem to be moving out of the period of secularizing and into a time in which the gifts of prayer and contemplation will once again be valued.

If Leech's picture of how various groups of people are focusing on matters of spirituality is impressionistic, it nevertheless corresponds to the path travelled by many of the people and institutions with which I have been in contact. Many were concerned two decades ago to discover a more secular presentation of the Christian faith and to describe models of transcendence that were discernible *within* life experience. At that time many Christians would not even have granted a need to engage with the transcendent at all.

The world no longer has to be flattened out; the high points, the peaks of our experience, are there to be scaled; and the journey into the realm of the religious is no longer to be avoided. The secularizing spiritualities of the 1960s proved, in the event, not to be what met the need; what is wanted is not, after all, to pray in the secular city, in the midst of everyday experience, but to seek by whatever means are available a road towards the discovery of God in personal religious experience. Whatever may have been the crises of faith that afflicted the intellectual community, it is now clear that there is still a real demand, if not a need, for what people can acknowledge as authentic religious experience.

It is also true, and Leech's book is a clear example of this, that there are those in the churches who are sure that it is the task of the Church to respond to that demand, and that the resources are available within the Christian tradition to do so. What is needed is a new concern for the spiritual aspect of Christian discipleship, and the recovery of the skills and practice of the spiritual life and of directing others in it. The subtitle of Tilden Edwards's book *Spiritual Friend* is 'Reclaiming the Gift of Spiritual Direction', and he is one example of the founding of a programme of training in spiritual direction so that the new and greater concern with spirituality can be met. It is perhaps the inevitable consequence of the increased interest that there should be established institutes and programmes of training to foster it. One wonders what the wise counsellors and confessors of earlier generations would have thought had they dreamt that in the future spiritual direction might turn into a professional discipline with a diploma to ensure standards. Those who establish such courses and institutes do so with the desire to meet a clearly expressed need of our time; yet their efforts can produce consequences which, from the standpoint of the Christian spiritual and pastoral tradition, seem to us bizarre.

I am not decrying the existence of a greater interest in spirituality; nor am I writing of it as a disinterested or distant observer, far less as a critic seeking to spit on it from a great height. I have been surprised, in view of the ideas with which I first entered the ministry, to find in myself an increased and increasing interest in the contemplative aspects of discipleship and a much greater wish than before to enable myself and others to grow in it. Partly that has been in response to the expressed needs of those who have sought ministry from me; they have been very important teachers to me. But that is not the whole story. I have been forced to acknowledge — and at times it has felt like an external constraint — that the discipleship of involvement in the life of the world is not all there is. Not only that; if that is all there is, it becomes another duty, weighed down with an 'ought' that deprives the involvement I seek of both its power and its spontaneity. In common with many others who have been exponents of a theology of liberation and a discipleship of social action, I have found myself increasingly aware of the ineffectiveness and burdensomeness of that kind of proclamation which pays no attention to our need of inner resources.

Nor is contemplation simply turning out to be necessary as a piece of self-equipping for a more vital task of involvement. For many exponents of liberation, prayer has turned out to be a subversive activity in its own right. It has been a parallel sign of God's care for the outcast that the service of God should include as a central aspect actions and insights, times and places, which are not directly productive even of those changes in the life of an unjust world which our times so urgently demand.

The move towards a greater willingness to engage with matters directly spiritual has come also from those who have concerned themselves with the study of human relations. There was a time when the study of group dynamics, the practice of human relations education and training in pastoral care and counselling represented a very secularizing tendency. The insights of psychotherapy and group dynamics were appropriated not merely as aids to pastoral practice and to the management of the life of the local church but by many as what Christianity was really all about. Salvation and psychological health became synonymous as goals for the individual, and a certain intensity and personal honesty were cultivated as marks of the Church at least as important as the sharing of the apostles' doctrine, the breaking of bread and the prayers. But Don Browning[1] is only the clearest example of those now insisting on the vital importance of the theological framework within which pastoral care is offered, and Bruce Reed[2] insists that the specifically religious nature of the Church's life is not only vital for those who participate in it but for the rest of the community as well. You do not have to belong to the Moral Majority or the Festival of Light to be part of a movement towards a greater explicitness about our religious heritage and a greater concern for the transcendent and how the sense of it can be experienced and offered.

And all this, say many, is not before time. Those who objected strongly to the theological currents of the 1960s are bound to feel vindicated and to be glad that what they must see as a greater balance in the proclamation of the gospel is being recovered. And they may be right; we may be doing better than our predecessors and at least making some sort of response to areas of need we used to ignore. The claims for secularity may have been premature, or overstated, or downright false. If the criticism of religion was widely heard as a criticism of all concern with prayer, and the demand for

'Christianity without religion' was understood as a demand for discipleship without worship, it may indeed have been because the terms were not well enough defined. It may also have been because among the protagonists of the new theology there was a greater concern with attacking 'other-worldliness' than with building patterns of devotional life that might answer their own criticisms.

It is possible, however, that our greater balance, our (perhaps) greater clarity and constructiveness about spirituality have been purchased at a price, and that something has been lost after all in exchange for what has been found. My reasons for wondering whether this is so are again highly impressionistic and subjective. The time of the secular theology was also one in which it was possible to cherish some concrete political hopes for the development of a society founded on justice and peace. Put like that, it is surprising that anybody could have been so naive; but it remains the case that enormous efforts, and costly ones, were put into striving for a world of inter-racial and international peace, as well as to see that the efforts to cushion the worst effects of poverty were maintained.

If the secular theologies are lying under a pile of debris, then I suspect that some of the debris is the ruins of those shattered political dreams. At least some of the new-found prayer is being offered in response to those ruins; certainly some of mine. Not only that. The loss of any sense that our societies might be moving corporately in the direction of a more just and humane order has been accompanied also by the devastating and painful ending of many personal relationships, marriages particularly, which were formed in times when personal honesty and intimacy were at a premium and when, therefore, it might have been supposed that relationships were built on foundations of some security. It seems not to have been so.

If much of the progress which liberals were hoping for has ground to a halt, it may of course produce some good in the end. Good may also emerge from many of the devastated personal relationships. There is no need to question that possibility, because it is not the point. The point is that the political and the personal devastation that many have experienced do give us cause to reflect whether our greater concern with prayer (and that is not always the same as our greater praying) is actually a journey inwards as we might want to think. Perhaps it is a journey backwards, or a flight outwards.

If we thought we had the impetus and the resources to make real changes in public affairs for the sake of justice and peace, and if we thought we had the skills to base personal relationships on greater honesty and integrity, that optimism is largely shattered. The shattering of that optimism is a crucial element in the environment in which whatever renewed concern there might be for the affairs of the spirit has to be understood. That does not make our concern less valid or less valuable; but if we do not take into account the environment and the effect which it is having upon us, we shall be very unlikely to make a really satisfactory contribution to meeting people's concern with prayer.

Many would find that suggestion surprising. Spirituality is, after all, concerned with the individual self; that much is clear. The outside world impinges on a person, offering stimulus, or excitement, or joy, or sadness or fear. These have to be contended with as a person engages in the spiritual life. They may get in the way of spiritual growth. They may offer subjects for prayer. The world and the changing moods of the individual who confronts the world may be agenda for sessions with a spiritual director. But they are not spirituality's basic material nor do they represent its main goal. On many understandings of what it is to engage with spirituality, the world is essentially a backdrop against which the personal struggle for meaning, for direction, for the awareness of God is to be conducted. On that basis, our aim for the world is that it should become a place which does not prevent the growth of people or their discovery of meaning for their lives. And if the world is to be changed at all, it can only be by the steady process of the conversion and growth of individuals.

On that understanding, any increase in concern for spirituality, for the life with God, is to be welcomed; and questioning the basis of that increased interest is cynical and inappropriate. What is required is more effective help for people in pursuing the resources of the spiritual life and training for those who might assist others in that growth. The 'politics' of our situation, its historical roots, may require tackling at some level; but that is a separate task. To pray is to pray; to meditate is to meditate. They are good activities to engage in, and the idea that you can have too much of a good thing, or indeed that there might be good and bad reasons for doing them, is to avoid the responsibility of offering some of the specific assistance and practical help that it is incumbent on the churches to give to those seeking it.

But even if the task of providing specific assistance and resources is acknowledged, there is no way of evading the question of what that assistance is thought to be for. It may be that prayer and meditation constitute essential elements in the health of the individual. Maybe to welcome a concern with prayer is to welcome the end of an era when it was thought that the resources of religion had little to contribute to personal wholeness, and the reaction of the organized churches is 'We told you so'. Personal health has spiritual as well as mental and physical components; the religious have always known this and are glad to discover that many who have not previously thought of themselves as religious are becoming aware of the fact as well. The believer may accept that God is concerned with our physical and mental well-being as well as our spiritual health, but spirituality has a particular place in God's attention — and a particular claim on ours if we want to attend to God.

Yet personal health is not in itself enough reason to be concerned with prayer. The question of purpose remains. You are fit — or unfit — *for* something. Health and fitness presuppose a certain understanding of what human life is for and to what end it is to be directed. We choose which physical and mental powers to develop according to some assumptions, often not expressed, about how we are to live, and what the experience of life is to be like. Disciplines which may fit us admirably for relaxation and tranquillity may fit us also for passionate engagement with intractable social conflict in the world or a sacrificial concern for the well-being of others; but then again they may actually unfit us. The prayers that belong to a context in which faith has to be a secret matter and changes in the order of society cannot be expected — as at a time of political repression — are hardly of the kind that will serve a time when lively and imaginative participation, for example in a revolutionary situation, is called for.

There is another oddness also about welcoming a concern with spirituality without asking questions about its context. I am assuming, and that means I am not going to devote space to arguing, that any talk about spirituality is talk about relationship with God, and that the God of Christian faith is believed to be concerned about the creation of a good, just and healthful context. That God, with whom our spirituality is supposed to sustain and enrich our relationship, has never given us to understand that the saving of individual souls is the only matter of divine concern or even that the survival or aggrandizement of the Christian Church itself is a sufficient end. The earth and the sea were not said to have been made as preparatory training exercises for a divine creator wishing to sharpen up skills in readiness for Friday's task of people-making; grain and mustard seeds are not there simply to supply material for parables; and the purpose of our bodies is not to provide a sufficiently difficult and tempting obstacle course out of which the souls destined for heaven might emerge.

And crucially and specifically to our concern here, the broad sweep of human history, its wars and recessions, its revolutions and oppression, have not been represented in our tradition as a roaring and turbulent sea allowed but ignored by a God who, when all is said and done, is really only interested in the drops of water left glistening on the sand (the sand only being there so that they will have something to glisten on). Of course Christians have not always spoken, let alone lived, as though context mattered; but when they have spoken or acted in a neglectful way towards the issues facing the world around us it has not been out of ignorance of the biblical and theological arguments that could be ranged against them. It was because they had other concerns, altruistic or otherwise, or because they were afraid or unimaginative.

When, on the other hand, Christians have decided to stop ignoring the social environment in which people live and instead to engage courageously with the powers of this world on behalf of society's victims, that too has not happened because somebody reminded them of the arguments which are to be found in the Bible. The renewal of our involvement comes out of a renewal of inspiration, not always sought or deliberately intended. Often we have been dragged reluctantly into whatever century it happened to be, propelled by some inescapable development, rather than by any particular conviction about what ought to be.

The problem therefore is not whether God is or is not interested in human history and whether we ought or ought not to be similarly involved. I am making the assumption that that issue is decided: there is no God who is not involved in the human story, and there is no service of God that is not concerned with that story. What is at issue is how we are to discover the interior resources — the courage, the imagination, the hope for the world — and how we are to overcome the interior barriers — the fear, the despair and the sense of powerlessness — so that involvement can happen. That is the issue about spirituality, and it is always the issue, whether or not it happens to be a time when the spirituality market is, so to speak, moving upwards. What kind of personal journey, what understanding of health of spirit, most profoundly enables commitment to fellow human beings and to a world of justice and peace? What are the prayers that most rightly accompany human righteousness and express belief in a God who refuses to be uninvolved in the world as it is?

Lest it should sound as though what is being advanced here is an understanding of spirituality that is purely utilitarian, and from which contemplation, silence and solitariness for their own sake are excluded, we need to be clear that the relationship between prayer and action is not, of course, a mechanical one. It is not that we pray or meditate in crder then to go off and act. There are those who claim that churchgoing is an opportunity to 'recharge one's batteries'. I am not suggesting that everything in the way of prayer is only justified by the action it leads to. There are, however, two kinds of life: life with integrity, where a common intention to love and to be just, to hope and above all to be committed pervades both our contemplation and our activity; and life without integrity where we learn Houdini's art of escape from activity just at the point where it might become serious and from silence just at the point where it might become demanding. It is that former alternative, life with integrity, that concerns us here.

That integrity is not something which all individuals have strenuously to seek to achieve in their own lives, considered by themselves. One of the most important insights of the current concern with spiritual direction is that individuals have different gifts, aptitudes and shortcomings, and have to find a pattern that is appropriate for them. Integrity is not a matter of conforming to some ideal notion of the balanced life. Integrity comes from the balance and interplay of the gifts and the passions of individuals who recognize that they are drawn in different directions from one another and who even in their disagreements have much to gain from one another. The notion that integrity is something to be achieved in the individual life is in fact a profoundly oppressive demand for conformity.

Nobody who has experienced the immense mutual contribution that is possible between those who live alone and the families with whom they come in contact, for example, could countenance the quite widespread notion, expressed in all sorts of social pressures, that singleness is some kind of disability. Equally, to have experienced the almost unbelievable power of those who have given their lives to contemplation or who have heard tell of what contemplatives gain from the activity of the world around them could possibly accept that it would be better if action and contemplation were only expressed as different aspects of the lives of individuals.

It is in fact the 'one-sided' patterns of life which others have chosen which enable us to focus on the questions that need resolving in our own lives. Our praying, no less than our action, has therefore a function in relation to the lives of other people at least as important as its function in our own. When we give ourselves to activity, or when we give ourselves to contemplation, we are also delegating, committing to others that to which we are not at that moment attending. The integrity we seek is one that we need to seek together, and just because spirituality is a fashionable concern it is important to attend to the discovery of that shared integrity. Otherwise it will be lost in the rush as individuals pursue an individualistic ideal of spiritual health and personal growth.

So the interior journey that people make, their spirituality, is bound up with their context as is the whole of their living. They may individually or as a society become more or less interested in that journey, and that increase or lessening of interest has roots that penetrate widely and deeply into what is happening in society at large. Individuals may be more or less interested than others in becoming aware of their interior landscape or in plumbing the resources of the traditions of contemplation or meditation. It may be offensive to those who are concerned with teaching or helping others with the life of prayer that it should be thought of as a hobby, like football, woodwork or collecting Chinese pottery, but there is that about it; individuals make their choice of interest or lack of it, the time they spend, the traditions they like and the rewards they look for. In the process they may realize that they are dealing with realities far more demanding of commitment than a mere hobby, but there is ample scope and evidence for variation in what individuals need and pursue in the way of spirituality.

It is that scope for individual variation, based on the temperament, the life experience, the educational background of individuals, that makes the task of assisting one another in coming to terms with our own interior journeys such a vital and rewarding one. There are many who find themselves deprived of any knowledge of even some of the five-finger exercises of a life which allows space for reflection, awareness and growth, let alone the richness and variety of religious traditions which include every kind of mystical experience and meditative skill. The need is there for those who can assist others to find their way or, even more creatively, to enable groups of people to function in a way that makes it possible for the individual members to explore, to journey and to be enriched. Yet the context in which individuals live and have to find their way is there to be embraced and not to be fled from. It is our world, our society, that to an overwhelming extent shapes our experience and that also seeks for justice and peace to reign. Those who seek a shape and a meaning for their own lives do so either as part of, or at the expense of, their struggle for a world without violence or oppression. Soul friends are also friends of the soul of the world or they are its enemies. Their advice and their shared exploration either assist the growth of the soul of the world or stand in its way. The discernment that is required of those who would grow in themselves includes a discernment of where they stand in the system of things, in an order which can oppress or set free — and which mostly oppresses.

The child stands erect, totters along, falls, cries, is picked up, ceases to cry and starts to walk again, upright as before. In doing so, the child repeats the experience of children of every generation and engages one of the earliest challenges that come to us all. That particular child exhibits the individuality of an inheritance of physique and of temperament that belongs to the child alone and has never belonged to anyone else.

But the child has a place in history and in the ordering of things that plays a crucial role even in that basic human experience. The room is spacious and the floor safe to fall on because the parents have space and money. The child is watched by someone with concern and time, and enough inner tranquillity to let the child be. He might have been watched by someone overwhelmed by life's pressures, whose own need to survive is barely met by available resources. The context is one in which safety and love can be transmitted; it might be one in which the entail of poverty and powerlessness simply gets passed on to the next generation. To be aware of those contextual issues is to be in a world in which nothing is irrelevant: environmental pollution, housing policy, the inequality of women and men, the life choices that are available to people whose schools are inadequate and whose streets are unsafe.

These political issues affect far more than our learning to walk. They alter the way we think, the way we learn to distinguish truth from falsehood and beauty from ugliness. People learn, for example, about keeping promises not only by what they are told but also by what they experience from their parents and from society at large. Are the promises implied and often expressed by the early affection and encouragement which children receive borne out in the opportunities made available to them at school and when school is finished? People hear that beauty is an important characteristic; but they notice that it appears not to matter if the area where they have to live is not beautiful at all. The environment which society gives to us crucially affects and sometimes completely determines our ability to receive and create trust, to show affection and to entertain hope.

Furthermore, our social environment is not simply the landscape in which prayer takes place. The environment, our own and other people's, the way we experience it and what we are prepared to do about it, are absolutely integral to the content and the value of our praying. The contrast Jesus makes between the prayer of the Pharisee and the prayer of the publican is not merely a contrast between two sets of words; it is a contrast between two lives and two sets of social relations. To call a magnificent choral Te Deum worship is to undertake to notice not simply the beauty of the singing but what you pay those who sing and the lengths to which you have to go to secure the building in which it takes place. The curses of prisoners are also prayers, and the prayers of the rest of us have to be judged in relation to the attention we give to what our society's outcasts are experiencing. That concern needs to take a variety of forms, including attention to the immediate needs they have as individuals, but not excluding the battery of forces and circumstances that have put them where they are.

The many diverse activities which are involved in caring for people, both the binding-up of their wounds and the enriching of their interior life, are our starting-point. Those activities have exerted a profound claim upon many in our society who find pastoral work deeply satisfying and enriching. This book is, however, concerned to show that that work can be immensely enriched if it is seen as a starting-point and a means to opening the eyes of those who engage in it to the full potential and pain of the world in which individuals have to find their way. Pastoral work and spiritual care are therefore an entry into the struggles of politics and of our fundamental attitudes to how human beings are meant to be and to be with each other. The activity of care which has been a core activity of the Christian community from its beginning opens out into concern for the public world which those who need our care demand we take notice of.

If we look not at others but at our own interior landscape

we shall also find clues about where we stand in the public issues of our day. We shall discover to what extent we are either surrendering or offering resistance to the oppressive powers at work in the world outside. Those clues can lead us to the place of opportunity, the place where it is possible to think of making a difference to the way things are and to empower those for whom we care also to make a difference to the world they inhabit. It is possible then to see the giving and receiving of pastoral care, as I have also experienced it, as something which increases our determination to express in the public world what we most aspire to for ourselves: a greater openness, a profounder affection, a more immediate sense of God's presence and God's will, and a hope to sustain us when that will seems a long way from fulfilment.

Let us unite, let us hold each other tightly, let us merge our hearts, let us create — so long as the warmth of this earth endures, so long as no earthquakes, cataclysms, icebergs or comets come to destroy us — let us create for Earth a brain and a heart, let us give human meaning to the superhuman struggle.[3]

THREE

The Fear of Adulthood

'Yes, sir.' I have never been so crushed by so respectful a remark. There cannot be anything worse than to have somebody agree to do what you say when you thought what you were learning about—and even getting better at—was being *non*-directive. I had been gradually learning more about the style and method of pastoral counselling associated with the name of Carl Rogers. The counsellor endeavours to listen to and reflect what the client is saying, so that the client can hear the message which is coming through. However, for me to think about spirituality and pastoral care involves confronting some of my more inglorious failures in understanding both myself and others. In this particular instance, the conversation that ended with this devastating piece of obedience illustrates only too well the difficulty of moving from passivity to activity or from acquiescence to rebellion. It illustrates also what happens when you attempt to apply the values that might be appropriate to your own situation to that of another, without any serious consideration of the entirely different context within which the other person has to choose his or her values and apply them.

The first thing to say about this conversation is that it took place in a prison between a member of the chaplaincy staff and an inmate. That is an essential aspect of the context. Bill had been seeing me regularly and we had, I supposed, an increasingly valuable relationship. The time was approaching for his release, and this conversation was about some of the preparations that needed (again, *I* supposed) to be made for that event. One by one issues came up: where to live, what friends might be there on the outside worth getting in touch with, what possibilities there might be for preparing for or seeking work. His expression became more and more blank and his tone of voice more and more apathetic as he recited his lack of thought about, let alone answers to, any of the questions which it seemed to me were the obvious ones to look at.

I had been moderately well schooled by this time in the outward and visible signs that were supposed to go with a non-directive manner on the one hand and a climate of warm and affirming attention on the other. The inner schooling, however, had yet to be made as effective for me. What I felt at that time was neither warmly attentive nor even slightly non-directive. I was frankly furious that the obvious was not being seen; and also that at just the point where the work we had done together might stand a chance of having value for the future, he appeared to have no energy left. Finally, the real presence of Carl Rogers forsook me. 'Don't you think', I said, 'that it's high time you did think about some of these things?'

I have already said what he replied. The words 'Yes, sir' were the words of obedience; the tone, as can be guessed, was totally apathetic and his expression was vacant. The conversation ended soon; I was overcome with a sense of futility and of *my* failure to notice the obvious. The end of a period of years in prison is no time to be told to take responsibility for your life. 'Law-abiding' society has removed from the prisoner both the need and the possibility of taking that responsibility. The prospect of being suddenly required to do that, with of course the threat of renewed imprisonment if one fails, must be truly terrifying. As a black prisoner, Bill can only have felt that leaving prison was like moving from one prison to another. Moving into responsibility requires more than being told to do so.

This account of a mishandled situation is offered here not as a prelude to some ideas about pastoral technique or about how it could have been handled better. That story is chiefly one about the loss of the state of irresponsibility and the terrors which that loss holds. For as long as a person is in prison, there is a perfect alibi for any action or misfortune. As you do not decide anything for yourself, the consequences are not your responsibility. As a pawn in somebody else's chess game, you have no investment in who wins. You learn the ropes, what is required to survive; but you acquire no practice in the exercising of choice or the formation of values of your own.

You do not have to be in prison for that to be true, although that is a particularly dramatic example. Wherever your life is constrained, there you have a perfect alibi; there you are not to blame for whatever happens. If others choose to constrain your life because you are black, or poor, or female, then they provide you with an excuse. You did not choose; you are not responsible. For me to be angry was fine; I had a key to the room, and so I could be angry for both of us. I have no idea what happened to Bill, but I am fairly certain that he will have found some way of persuading society to put him in a place where once again his alibis will be perfect and where he will have no decisions to take on his own behalf.

The numbers who return to prison after discharge are a continuing testimony to the difficulty of regaining a hold on the capacity to be in charge of one's own life once that hold has been lost. They also are a witness to the immense difficulty we all experience in finding any imaginative way of dealing with those who insist that incarceration is preferable to freedom. There are very few rebellions as successful as the rebellion against responsibility; you can usually get somebody to take your decisions for you and to feel, as they co-operate in taking away liberty and responsibility, that they are, however reluctantly, doing what you need.

In my encounter with Bill we are presented with the terror of 'coming of age'. There is not as much talk about the coming of age of humankind as there was twenty years ago and indeed we seem very ready to turn our backs on much that was implied in our having attained adulthood. The burdens of technical advance seem to be feeling too heavy and there are many signs of our crying 'Stop'. Political ideologies which stress the possibility of planning for change are, on the whole, in retreat and it is attractive to many to regain our alibis, blaming past generations or impersonal abstractions like 'the recession' for our troubles.

It is possible that those who sought to celebrate our coming of age in the theological statements produced during the 1960s spoke prematurely, or overstated their case. Yet in one important respect they performed a service of lasting value. They pointed us again to the writings, and particularly the later writings, of Dietrich Bonhoeffer. His writing of our 'coming of age' was not grounded in some facile optimism, a fond belief that human beings would always make the right choices. His perception was deeply rooted in his own life experience and in the history through which he lived.

His life through the early decades of this century was full of immense promise as the gifts he had of warmth, leadership and intellect developed. His life story,[1] as it moved through academic formation, through becoming a pastor, into his position of leadership in the Confessing Church, constituted a movement step by step into that position for which he is famous, that of conspirator against Hitler and finally his victim. It is as though each moment in that life story and each new turn of his thought were the unwitting preparation for ideas that were to bring him into final conflict with authority and in the process bring to birth ideas which we still have not sufficiently assimilated. His story was also deeply intertwined with the tragedy of the Nazi period. As the German people opted for the principle of the leader as expressed by Hitler, so Bonhoeffer began by finding that principle contrary to the understanding of constitutional order in which he had been brought up. Then as time went on he saw it as contrary to God's redemptive purpose as revealed in the gospel. Finally he was driven to the gravest decision of all, that of taking part in the plot to assassinate Hitler.

This unfolding vocation bears a remarkable resemblance to the way in which Bonhoeffer described the coming of age of humankind in his *Letters and Papers from Prison.* For he was not speaking about human maturity as we understand the term, far less about a society which is likely to make the right choices when offered them. It can hardly have escaped the notice of one who was locked in a Nazi cell that human beings do not always make good choices or act with maturity. Yet his experience had been a parable of the way in which, as ideas develop and a life story moves on, suddenly and unexpectedly the ideas learned in previous years present themselves, like a cheque to be cashed, as ideas which require action and sacrifice and which allow no escape.

The possibilities of space in which to develop thought and the security for an expansive and full life about which he could write so movingly, disappeared. That is the experience of humanity as he then all too briefly but powerfully described it. What he was clear about was the demise of alibis, and specifically the alibis furnished by religion. Coming of age,

Mündigkeit, is not something you deserve or earn or necessarily enjoy; it is simply a fact that at a certain point you come of age and have to answer for yourself. You sign your own cheques and incur your own debts, you answer for your own crimes and have to keep your own promises because there is nobody else who can be asked to keep them for you. You are responsible, accountable and without excuses to plead. There are no tests to determine whether you have reached this stage, except the test of age. What Bonhoeffer claimed was that the human race had now reached such a stage in its development, whether it liked its new stage or not and whether it deserved it or not.

The secularizing theologies of the 1960s interpreted Bonhoeffer as having made some very optimistic claims about the capacity of human beings to handle the world in which they live in a mature way without recourse to religion. The world's coming of age was therefore grounded in the maturity of the human race. It is true, of course, that for Bonhoeffer the coming of age of the world is grounded in certain developments which can be described as human achieve-ments, not, as in the coming of age of an individual, simply in the passage of time. But the achievements are not anything to do with psychological maturity and the proven capacity to make unaided moral judgements. They are not, that is to say, the kind of achievements as a result of which humankind might be said to deserve to manage by itself. The achieve-ments are those of knowledge and of science which make it increasingly necessary for us to live without recourse to God.

> The movement that began about the thirteenth century . . .
> towards the autonomy of man (in which I should include
> the discovery of the laws by which the world lives and
> deals with itself in science, social and political matters, art,
> ethics and religion) has in our time reached an undoubted
> completion. Man has learnt to deal with himself in all
> questions of importance without recourse to the 'working
> hypothesis' called 'God'. In questions of science, art and
> ethics this has become an understood thing at which one
> now hardly dares to tilt. But for the last hundred years or
> so it has also become increasingly true of religious
> questions; it is becoming evident that everything gets along
> without 'God' — and, in fact, just as well as before.[2]

Clearly it is possible to question much here as a matter of historical judgement, and it is easy enough to brand it as an oversimplification. As we have already noted, there is in fact a resurgent interest in all kinds of religion and religious experience. It is certainly hard to agree that the movement of which Bonhoeffer speaks has in our time reached 'an undoubted completion'. The reality of our situation is much more complicated than that, and this is particularly true if we take seriously the fact that white and western nations constitute a small part of the world scene; what has happened to our society is by no means a universal phenomenon, and it would be a brave person who would predict with any certainty that it will become so.

In any case, if we take seriously the model of the coming of age in a person's life as well as our experience of historical development, we have to say that coming of age is not a once-and-for-all development. The process of taking responsibility and of finding ourselves in charge is one that is repeated as the years pass and new experiences come to us. At one stage we find ourselves responsible, say, as parents and experience the daunting realization that whoever may be there to help, in the end the responsibility is ours. But then, as children grow up, we find we are mistaken to hold on to that responsibility and instead a new one comes upon us, appropriate to the next stage in our lives. It was not that we were mistaken in the responsibility we thought had come upon us, but that new times demand new forms of coming of age.

It is similar with the movement of civilization. Knowledge advances and new ideas are explored and in the process new responsibilities dawn upon us and alibis disappear. Yet the process is a continuing one and is never 'complete'. Responsibilities appear to burden us for a time and then disappear to be replaced by new demands. Scientific exploration led to the splitting of the atom; it was a responsible choice at the time, but it opened up such a range of issues as to lead many to regret the choice had been made. Yet choices cannot be unmade and humanity cannot retake the decisions which have led it to the present. So the experience of coming of age is a repeated and repeating experience of the death of alibis and the appearance of new burdens. It is never over and done with.

All these criticisms can be made of Bonhoeffer's claim that the world is 'come of age'. But when all the criticisms have been made, we are still left with the sense that his major prophetic point cannot be avoided. We may not get along very well without God, but as a matter of fact we find ourselves living most of the time as though that was indeed what we have to do. It is not only that most scientific exploration proceeds most of the time without the slightest recourse to the hypothesis of God; it is also that the more intractable our problems are, the more we find ourselves driven to the conclusion that however much we might like it to be true that there is Someone who would intervene to solve them, in reality we have simply to get on with solving them on our own. If war is to be avoided, it must be by the difficult and drawn-out processes of negotiation. If the blight that affects the rundown areas of our cities is to be remedied, it will require government action or more investment or a change in the housing policies. If the economics of growth turn out to have had their day, our society will have to find ways of adjusting to that or use our ingenuity to create a stable economy based on finite resources. There is no Someone who will do that job for us; there is nowhere to look for the answers to the hard questions, no book of life with the correct solutions provided by an omniscient God.

It is not just the survival of churches which is made doubtful by such a world view; the demand that we should believe as adults is also very threatening for individual Christians. We often think that a return to a world in which dependence upon God came more naturally would be preferable. Our hope is that we can demonstrate a continuing need for religion by reference to those questions which every human being has to face but which the advance of human knowledge has not solved.

> Efforts are made to prove to a world thus come of age that it cannot live without the tutelage of 'God'. Even though there has been surrender on all secular problems, there still remain the so-called 'ultimate questions' — death, guilt — to which only 'God' can give an answer, and because of which we need God and the church and the pastor.[3]

Bonhoeffer asks what will happen to this attempt to retain

the world's dependence on God if the time comes when even these ultimate questions do not exist as such; if, that is, we find ways of dealing with them 'without God'. Certainly the growth of human knowledge has in no sense resolved the 'ultimate' questions of guilt and death, but there is no question that both those issues have been made to look very different in the light of the human and medical sciences. Even those who handle death and guilt as religious problems do so in the light of what secular knowledge has taught us about such questions as dealing with pain, the processes of grieving and 'pathological' or 'unhelpful' manifestations of guilt. The 'ultimate' questions are not much of a refuge, in any case. It is a much attenuated God who bears rule only at the boundaries of human existence and is banished from within it. What kind of belief is it, in any case, that regards the questions of an individual's guilt or death as ultimate questions which remain in the hands of God while treating the possibility of a nuclear holocaust or devastating conflict between rich and poor as matters of purely secular concern and therefore of *pen*ultimate significance or less importance?

There are also, for Bonhoeffer, and there need to be for us, serious moral questions about a kind of religious belief that seeks to capitalize on, and even encourage, human weakness. He regards any attempt, be it religious or secular, to compromise the adult status of human beings as

> in the first place pointless, in the second place ignoble, and in the third place unchristian. Pointless, because it seems to me like an attempt to put a grown-up man back into adolescence, i.e. to make him dependent on things on which he is, in fact, no longer dependent, and thrusting him into problems that are, in fact, no longer problems to him. Ignoble, because it amounts to an attempt to exploit man's weakness for purposes that are alien to him and to which he has not freely assented. Unchristian, because it confuses Christ with one particular stage in man's religiousness, i.e. with a human law.[4]

We must not underestimate the challenge presented by Bonhoeffer's criticism of a religion that seeks to base itself on the weakness of people. The presentation of the gospel has, of course, to meet its hearers at some point that makes a

connection with their lives. It might come as a challenge to
repentance or an invitation to undertake new acts of service
or heroism. It might offer hope for a better future. Such
presentations would call on the hearers to give of their
strength. Yet the history of the preaching of the gospel
suggests that it has generally been presented not as a
summons to strength but as a remedy for weakness.

In particular, our sinfulness and our mortality have most
often been the soil in which the seeds of faith have been
planted, so that many would find it difficult to believe that
there ever could be a presentation of the faith that did not
meet us at those two points. And they are, of course, points of
vulnerability and weakness. The stance before God of the
sinner in need of forgiveness is not just one among many
possible stances that have been taken: it is the pre-eminent
stance that has characterized the religious. They may wish to
give thanks for health and strength, family and friends; but
the context of their thanksgiving seems overwhelmingly to be
the sense of personal release, redemption, forgiveness and
inspiration. These religious concerns are not chosen by
believers in some cynical attempt to find a last ditch in which
God can be defended so as to avoid the pain of giving up on
belief completely. The process is altogether more unconscious,
and altogether more inescapable.

The burden of the world Bonhoeffer describes — so
accurately, in my view — is almost beyond bearing. The
steady growth of our human knowledge and our human
power propels us in a direction that in part we acknowledge
as release, but in part we detest. That way lies endless
decision-making, the knowledge of how much we could
change if only we would make the effort, and of the dire
consequences for the human race if we do not. And there is in
the end nobody upon whom the responsibility can be shuffled
off. The buck stops with the human race, not because we
chose to take all the power to ourselves in some majestic act
of pride but because, under the impact of our own steadily
growing capacities to explore, to understand and then to
conquer, there was nowhere else to go. We went gradually
forward, our speed of movement increasing, until one day we
woke up and it was so: we were here with voice and vote on
the committee of millions who will decide whether there is to

be a next generation and what it will be like to belong to it.

Human beings are apt to feel a measure of relief that there are some human experiences, like death, which stand for the fact that we cannot decide everything for ourselves and indeed do not have to. Even professed atheists, who claim that human beings have no need of a God to depend on and who see religion as a primitive survival, can find themselves questioning at times whether adulthood is all liberation. We vary in the welcome we give to our come-of-age status; most of the time we want to try to change things for the better and see it as our responsibility to do so, and some of the time we address ourselves, with a mixture of anger and relief, to the areas of living about which there seems to be nothing that can be 'done'.

That takes us right back to Bill and me in the prison, to my anger and his 'Yes, sir'. The roots of what seemed like his totally apathetic response are complex, and certainly I was aware of my pastoral ineptitude. And with a bit of learning and a bit more time we might have managed to get to the point where my handling of the situation would have improved somewhat and his response would have moved ever so gradually in the direction of a capacity to make some life choices. At the very best he might even have come to the point of preferring liberty to prison. There is scope for action that might result in the creation of some support systems for people in Bill's situation. That also might make his return to prison a little less inevitable. It is vitally important that such systems of support should be created wherever possible. We also need to explore and become much clearer about what the meeting of such a person with a Christian pastor might hope to achieve in enabling both of them to understand and experience more fully together what forgiveness, faith, hope, love and the grace of God might mean in that situation. That is to say, we have to find ways of responding in circumstances which represent, among other things, a crisis for the human spirit and a desperate challenge to faith for both the people involved.

Yet before we rush into those activities and discussions, as at some point we must, and before we become too easily convinced that pastoral training and prisoners' after-care with a course in spiritual direction are the only responses we can make, we need to stay with the experience of anger and apathy a little longer, noticing and experiencing those things for what they are, anger and apathy. The pastoral encounter which I have described is indeed a pastoral encounter, but it is also a human experience that exposes realities deeper than can be dealt with by means of the pastoral care of one individual for another or of improved after-care. Our environment, our context also cries out for attention. If we do not look at what the anger and the apathy have to tell us about the context in which Bill and I are meeting, and instead rush to 'cure' them, our care will be shallow and ultimately unhelpful.

The two of us are placed in a situation in which we are united even at the same time as we are divided. We are two human beings, of age, but compelled to be infants together. I am supposed by those who put me there to know what is best and to try to get this prisoner to see what is best before his release from prison. My feelings are those of the child furious at a friend who will not play; his are those of the friend who has tried all the toys that I am so anxious for him to play with, and knows they are all broken. Put like that, it becomes quite clear which of the two of us knows more about the reality of the situation in which we find ourselves, a situation in which we are not actually friends but are enemies on opposite sides of prison bars and racial discrimination. To be aware of that is to be in the position of asking what it would be like to stop pretending. Not to be aware of it, as I was not until it was too late, is not only to pretend but also to collude. However effective may be the skills of pastoral care, however strong may be our communication of the resources of faith, the plain realities of the bars and the discrimination remain — indeed, the more effective the treatment the more effective may be the self-deception. It might well be that at the end of an honest communication about those realities, if that could ever happen, we would still decide that the appropriate questions did concern in the immediate term the specific issues of hostel accommodation, sources of money, the location of friends and the possibility of employment. But we should have decided as adults to deal with the situation in that way because that was all, or the most, or the best that could be done, or because the alternatives were beyond us.

We might find ourselves walking erect, to use our earlier image, or falling, but we would not be cultivating a stoop and calling ourselves upright.

In that process we might also have learned a little more about Christ and the world come of age. Bonhoeffer, in the letter from which I have already quoted, affirms the insight of liberal theology in accepting the power of a secular view of the world; liberal theology does not seek to turn the clock back in the direction of a triumphalist religion that denies the achievement of human knowledge, nor does it regard sheer obscurantism as the appropriate response to the advance of learning. What Bonhoeffer criticizes in liberal theology — and his criticism has a very contemporary ring about it — is that it willingly accepts for Christ the place on the edge of existence that advancing secularity has left open. That is the place of our private concerns and our so-called ultimate questions. The world of human advance has no quarrel with a religion that seeks to quiet our personal fears, determine our personal morality (as long as it leaves others to determine theirs) and gives us the inner ability to tolerate intolerable situations, be they the ultimate enemy of death or the degradations imposed on the weak by an oppressive society.

Such a religion would lend itself well to our prisoner on the brink of discharge and to the person appointed to pastor him. It accepts the total secularity — the unaccountability before God — of the prison, the housing department and the job market. It seeks to offer refuge for the spirit in the midst of the intolerable and at best some assurance that the outward circumstances ranged against a person need not be ultimately destructive of value and self-respect. In enabling him to have a way of dealing with his inner disturbance, his fear and his guilt, and to recover some inner tranquillity, that kind of religion also suggests both to those who propound it and to those who hear it that it is those areas of inner disturbance that actually constitute Bill's problem.

All counselling and casework approaches can tend in that way to individualize problems. They transmit the assumption that the best a distressed person can hope for is to acquire the ability to adapt with less distress to circumstances that cannot be changed. When Christians counsel, there is the further risk that the great themes of the gospel, salvation, sin, forgiveness, are similarly individualized; God becomes one who holds us accountable for our inability to fit in and offers to 'treat' us with forgiveness and grace to conform. Such a God leaves unaccountable and untreated the dynamics of a society in which some are firmly locked into the position of victim in the simultaneous cycles of racism, poverty and homelessness, and end up assuming a totally disproportionate share of the accommodation that is made available to them in prisons and mental hospitals. The private lot of the prisoner would have been alleviated, and at the same time society assisted in loading on to him the continuing demand to conform which it loads upon all those whose power to take charge of their lives has been wrecked by economic or physical coercion of whatever kind. We expect depressingly similar things of the 'good' discharged prisoner, the 'good' worker, the 'good' child, the 'good' woman, the 'good' pupil. In the wake of the coming of age of the world there has emerged, for as long as Christians will accept it, a most baleful division of labour: the public arena is left to its own unchallenged devices while God is known at the edges by adherents who sustain themselves spiritually and offer to ameliorate pastorally the worst sufferings of the world's victims.

Christ and the world come of age, however, require a quite different kind of discipleship and therefore a different kind of care and sustinence. What Bonhoeffer sees as God's being edged out of the world is a real defeat, a real crucifixion. That defeat is not to be mitigated by a desperate search for boundary areas, places where there may be a small continuing domain left for God and where human beings are willing to abase themselves, if the small domain is small enough, and become like children in need of care and protection. Christ is known in a world come of age by those who take the adulthood of the world seriously enough to seek to struggle in the public life of the world for that which their faith leads them to believe the world is meant to become. They therefore participate in God's continuing experience of loss and defeat as reality and not merely as image or fantasy. Such adult discipleship in an adult world involves all the creativity and intelligence we can bring to bear on the unrighteousness of the world, and a continuing experience of real defeat, real tears and real frustration as we encounter a power in that unrighteousness that exceeds our worst imaginings. Real defeat, real falling to the floor in the middle of the room, is the likely experience of those who refuse on God's behalf to be bought off with a children's corner where the images and vocabulary of the struggle for the reign of God are present but the reality is never allowed to encroach.

Two prisoners have appeared in this chapter, and on the face of it they could not be more different. The one is known as a hero and a martyr whose writings have sold thousands of copies and whose theological agenda continues to excite large numbers of Christians. The other is someone unlikely ever to be heard of again, destined, we may suppose, to be a series of entries in a prison file. Dietrich Bonhoeffer, coming as he did from a professional background, chose to give himself in a cause we all salute: the defeat of Nazism. Bill, it would appear, coming from a poor black family, had never been able to make any choices at all.

Yet the reflections of Dietrich Bonhoeffer about the coming of age of humankind, with its opportunities and its burdens, are modelled in a remarkable way by his own fate and by the paralysis felt by Bill at the prospect of having to take charge of his own life again on release from prison. Taking charge, being responsible for one's environment, will not always have the dramatic consequences that it had for Bonhoeffer, and yet Bill's fear is surely an accurate representation of what happens to human beings, and to humanity as a whole, when the awesome decisions of life in the world have to be faced.

Pastoral encounters are always opportunities to see the wider context. They are opportunities, that is to say, not only to see the way in which social and political pressures are affecting the lives of individuals: they also offer some insight into the situation of humanity as a whole, and they unfold before us something of humanity's situation before God. That situation, which I am describing in Bonhoeffer's terms as 'come of age', poses challenges which are indeed extremely daunting.

The insights which pastoral encounters give us about society at large and about our situation in relation to God may not always be an appropriate focus for our attention while we are actually involved in the pastoral encounter. I recall Mike, an inmate of this same prison, who was clear

that his problems were due to the British presence in Ireland
and that on discharge his first task would be to go and fight
the British; in his case there was a great deal of evidence that
his wider revolutionary interests were an escape from what
were bound to be the much more routine, and much more
difficult, realities of his life.

Yet even if we decide that in any particular encounter we
must focus on the individual needs of the person before us
and not on the wider issues which that person's plight raises,
the insight and the viewpoint are still there. The political
realities which lie behind any individual's distress may be far
too daunting to face or they may not be an appropriate focus
for our attention at the time. But daunting or not, attended to
or not, the links between personal distress and a world of
injustice, between an individual's sense of meaninglessness
and the crisis of faith that arises from the adulthood of the
world, are there.

We pray, we counsel, we care within the historic struggles
of humanity and not apart from them. We arrive in each
other's presence with an agenda that may be taken up with
issues of hopelessness or emptiness, anxieties about marriages
or our children and fears for our health or our dying. But that
agenda is formulated within a history which requires us to
act our age and to be responsible for the world we inhabit and
the society which we have inherited, and it is in the light of
that task that the appropriateness of my anger, Bill's apathy,
Mike's revolutionary intentions, or Bonhoeffer's resistance
have to be assessed. And if those responses, or any of them,
are found to be inappropriate, it must be for some better
reason than that life feels better when we are not angry or
apathetic and is safer when we do not resist. Our encounters
reveal the way in which the counselling room is perpetually
invaded by the world outside.

To be aware of that invasion is to be invited into a world in
which neither humane ideals nor the love of God bear rule
even in theory; to move into that world erect and strong; and
to experience the reality of whatever fall may come in what
Bonhoeffer calls the defeat of God at the hands of a godless
world. That is an invitation not to be too content with the
creation of either a humaneness or a religiousness that can
only survive in the situation of what we are pleased to call a

pastoral encounter, or a sense of tranquillity and even wholeness that can only exist within the meditative or contemplative spaces we are able to create for ourselves. Indeed, there may be a tension between that engagement and its inevitable results and what we seek to make for ourselves in the realm of spirituality and pastoral care. To watch the effect on people of engagement with the forces of the world can indeed be terrifying. To engage in the campaign for nuclear disarmament or the ordination of women, or any other part of the struggle for justice and peace, is to experience the threat, and sometimes the reality, that one's life or that of one's friends, though not ended like Bonhoeffer's, will suffer deep wounds to self-esteem, relationships or personality. Those wounds will be attributed by those ranged against you to your immaturity or your inner disturbance, as Dag Hammarskjöld so tellingly writes:

> The courage not to betray what is noblest in oneself is considered, at best, to be pride. And the critics find their judgement confirmed when they see consequences which, to them, must look very like the punishment for a mortal sin.[5]

Bonhoeffer is a sign of what the consequences of engagement can be; Bill is a sign that the world's injustice shows itself in the damaged lives of individuals too paralysed to take charge of their lives. To provide care and spiritual refreshment for one another is to share in the world's superhuman struggle to face the tasks of adult existence. If we are aware of that, we shall be open to finding in our pastoral encounters our invitation to keep God company in God's hour of defeat.

FOUR

Therapy and Gospel

If I keep from meddling with people, they take care of
themselves.
If I keep from commanding people, they behave themselves.
If I keep from preaching at people, they improve themselves.
If I keep from imposing on people, they become themselves.

LAO-TZE[1]

We live in the aftermath of a revolution in human self-
understanding. We can call it the explosion of awareness, an
era of massive preoccupation with introspection, a time of
unprecedented optimism about the capacity we have to
become what we are really meant to be. All of us who live in a
world that has been affected by the investigations of Freud
know that the world, our interior world as well as the exterior
world, can never be the same again. We are not of course all
Freudians; the kind of concern with the human self which he
unleashed has been taken in a whole range of different
directions, and the extent to which Freud himself was
influenced by his own cultural and historical context in the
conclusions he reached is a matter of great debate. But none
of us is immune from the effects of a developing belief in
people as being able (if they can come to terms with all that
has suppressed their true potential) to realize themselves, to
grow, to increase their capacity to love, to be aware of the
beauty and possibilities in the world around them — and in
fact to do a host of things which were denied to them when
they were slaves to cultural oppression, to parents or teachers
who told them how they ought to live.

   In that process a whole new battery of concepts has
emerged and the ones we had before have changed their

meaning. Knowing ourselves is not just about assessing in a commonsense way what is the reality of our gifts and shortcomings; to know ourselves is now to have gone on a journey inwards that will take us into the unresolved tensions and conflicts of years gone by, to turn over the stones that represent the values we thought we had accepted, and discover, and even find some affection for, the creepy-crawlies that lurk underneath them. We have all been told, and not just some of us, that loving one's neighbour as oneself requires that we should first love ourselves, and that requires that we should first know ourselves — and most of us have accepted the assumption that this means that the more we know ourselves the more we can love ourselves; and the more we can love ourselves the more we can love other people. So the second great commandment in the law, to love our neighbours as ourselves, is felt to result not in a series of moral attitudes, let alone legal provisions about how we are to behave with one another, but in processes of heightened awareness, in greater emotional freedom, in a capacity and a desire to know more and to feel more about one another. Obviously, the understanding of 'loving ourselves' which in one way or another has affected us all was not there at the time when that commandment found its way into the Book of Leviticus; nor for that matter would Jesus in quoting it have been party to that understanding of self-affirmation which we now take for granted. Our understandings of child-rearing and education all assume that it is damaging for people not to know and value themselves enough. And since all things come under the influence of the belief in growth, the belief that knowledge is a good thing leads on to the belief that more knowledge is a better thing; if an apple a day keeps the doctor away, eat two apples and you will never even need a Band-Aid! So a world in which there is more knowing and more loving is a world in which there will be more healing; there will be less fear and therefore less self-interested struggle for survival; there will be less war and oppression too.

I hold that we have all been affected in our attitude to our inner selves by this revolution in self-understanding whether we regard ourselves as part of that revolution or not. The most ardent devotees of the newest of the new psycho-therapies or growth movements and those who have not heard of any such things, or dislike what they have heard, or who consider that the sharing of feelings is a trespass on appropriate human reserve, may disagree strongly with each other. But they share a world view very different from that of previous generations. We all attach far more importance to our inner experience than did our forebears.

This change has been neither accidental nor arbitrary, certainly not confined to one social class, to the more narcissistic members of society or to recent emigrants to the west coast of the USA. We have arrived at this point because of the inexorable process of 'coming of age', in this case in relation to our inner selves. They are no longer an uncharted mystery to be accepted without question; they come within the sphere of our responsibility, where we *have* to take charge of our own lives because we *can* do so. We now know that the world of our feelings, our illusions, our values and our fundamental character is susceptible to manipulation by chemicals, by electrical charges, by hypnosis, by meditation, by brainwashing, and by a host of encounter methods from one-to-one psychotherapy to training seminars of 250 people. The source of our changed attitude to our inner world is fundamentally the same as the source of the nuclear age in which we also have to live: we have explored both the atom and the human mind; we have opened both up, and behold! — we are suddenly in new territory with new power and therefore fewer alibis; we have to make a decision about what to do, rather than just accept the givenness of what is. If we can alter the working of the human mind, why then, let us see which is the best way to do it and what are the results of doing it.

It is not surprising that many find this a fearful development. Baring one's soul and receiving confidences from others are situations particularly vulnerable to our ambiguous human motives. There is something intoxicating about revealing all or seeing all in a setting of intimacy and trust. The best possible intentions can be invaded by the unacknowledged needs of the carer. The possibilities of manipulation, knowing and unknowing, are immense and it would be a very brave person who claimed that the explosion of interest in counselling has not brought in its train an intoxication which has not always been easy to evaluate. Yet whatever the dangers have been, the testimonies to healing and growth are widespread, too widespread to be ignored. A valuable tool has been found here and we cannot now avoid the fact that we live in a world in which we are in charge of our inner selves as well.

One of the casualties of our taking charge of our inner selves is the philosophical truism that 'is' does not imply 'ought'. However impeccable may be the logic, that statement does not at all reflect the way in which altered possibilities create altered values. 'I'm your trainer,' says Don to the assembled 250 trainees in an EST (Erhard Seminar Training) seminar. 'I'm here because my life works, and you're here because your lives don't work.'[2] That Don's statement can be made in that setting at all indicates that our sense of what 'ought' to be is on the move. For a life to 'work' now includes the ability to feel in charge, to feel fulfilled in our relationships, to feel that the courses of action we embark on are ones we have really chosen, not merely acquiesced in because of values imposed on us as children, or which hold us back because we are afraid to change. Communication between people now works — or it does not — not simply at the level of semaphore signals which can be seen from ships at a distance, but at a profounder level where the whole person meets the other. Behind the word 'works', a word that seems clearly factual, lies a whole set of values which determine the directions we pursue about a wide range of public and private decisions. In response to this change, we have altered the way we bring up children, the kind of learning we expect in schools, the kind of marriage to which we aspire or which we are prepared to tolerate. We make huge demands on ourselves in the sphere of authenticity, understood as congruence between what we do and what we feel. Under the impact of the quest for this authenticity, all kinds of previously accepted duties come up for re-examination. We do not pursue careers because of some previously conceived expectation that we should do so if that turns out to be preventing us from 'being ourselves'; if we notice that some social norm is exercising dominance over us because we have not freely assented to it, we are quite likely to throw it over. If we find that our marriage refuses us the opportunity for the zest and creativity we have experienced in deep encounter with others we shall be willing, even at the cost of great pain, to give that zest and creativity a higher priority for ourselves than our marriage vows or our children.

This new world has often been described as permissive, but in reality there is not much that is permissive about it. We breathe the air of concern with our inner selves as inevitably as we breathe the air of oxygen and nitrogen, and exhaust fumes. Often it is those most unwilling to embark on any systematic personal exploration, those who would regard psychotherapy as dangerous or unnecessary who are sneaked up on by realities inside themselves that they did not know were there. Those unconscious longings are brought to the surface by some profound experience of communication or of an unexpected new relationship which, once experienced, will not go away. Like a coming of age it happens unasked and often unheralded, but when it happens there is a new world of responsibilities and difficult choices. There is also a new world of exhilaration and power, but that is not the reality that first presents itself. The new world offers choices that we did not have before, but what we have no choice about is whether we live in the world where those choices have to be made.

The values which characterize that new world include the belief that our inner world is important, and also that in a climate of sufficient trust and affirmation that world can be accessible to us so that we can have a new depth of awareness and new opportunities for choosing the direction of our lives. Carl Rogers writes:

> Individuals have within themselves vast resources for self-understanding, and for altering their self-concepts, basic attitudes and self-directed behaviour; these resources can be tapped if a definable climate of facilitative psychological attitudes can be provided.[3]

These words have parallels in the thinking and writing of a whole range of modern psychotherapies and are basic not only to his own non-directive counselling but to the understanding of people and their growth to which the advent of the human sciences has given rise. Freed from the wounds which have been inflicted on us through our upbringing and encounter with society, the inherent goodness, love and creativity of each of us can be free to flower.

Such a view of personhood, for that in the end is what it is, is a very strong challenge to much in the Christian tradition and presentation of what it is to be human. It is possible to put the force of that challenge in a shorthand way in a series of pairs of propositions, the first in each pair being what might have been gathered from traditional Christian presentations, the second being ideas undergirding or emerging from our contemporary concern with people's growth in authenticity and wholeness:

A.1 Humanity is fallen, flawed; that is part of what it is to be human and it is beyond sheerly human power to remedy.

A.2 The capacity of human beings to achieve boundless resources of love and creativity is limited only by the wounds inflicted on them through their encounter with the world; it is humanly possible, given sufficient resources of love and attention, to heal those wounds.

B.1 Because of the fallenness of humanity the constraint of a moral law is essential to save us from the consequences of our inner impulses.

B.2 The constraints of the morality and social conventions which are laid on us, and which we come to take upon ourselves as though they were our own, frequently isolate us from our real selves. Only self-discovery can lead to the choice of values that are really ours.

C.1 When we become aware that our lives do not match up to the values which we believe to be the right ones, the proper response is repentance, a turning back towards the direction in which we should be going, and a seeking of forgiveness for the past.

C.2 When we become aware of lack of congruence in our living we need to enter deeply into the experience of discomfort for long enough to discover its source, without prejudicing what we ought to be feeling or experiencing.

This polarized expression is related to ideas and not to people who hold them. It is to point up a tension, not to divide adherents into camps. Most people in reality live and think eclectically, taking ideas from a number of traditions, and certainly Christians who have involved themselves extensively in counselling or in human relations education have sought to play down those aspects of their Christianity which appear to be, or have been presented as being, demeaning of the intrinsic value or goodness of people as they are. But the tension remains. Confession and counselling are not, after all, the same kind of human activity; they require a different kind of assistance and a different attitude to the strengths and the weaknesses of people, and very often we have to make choices for ourselves, or in relation to people whom we are seeking to help, about which direction we are to take.

Philip, a man in his early thirties, is speaking with me about the pattern of his life and about his experience of prayer. He comes over as a person with a great number of abilities and a very inquiring mind. He has been taught various disciplines of prayer from his youth and finds them on the whole unsatisfactory. He senses a lack of discipline about his life and has great swings of mood from excitement to boredom and back again. He has had a fair bit of experience in counselling and in working in small groups, and has taken the opportunity that kind of work provides to learn more of himself. He finds himself about as interesting as he finds anything else, if anything slightly more so. He seems to be a person watching himself running along at the same time as running — and since it is quite difficult to do both at once it is usually the running itself that gets lost. Our conversations have a lassitude to them and an emotional detachment that rarely disappears.

I find myself responding to that lassitude and detachment by looking through the range of solutions I have to offer and the methods for dealing with such a situation. What will enable him, I ask myself, to become the vital and energetic person he needs to be if the whole range of his evident talents are to be used? And how can his religious belief and the resources for spirituality which it offers be available to him in the process of coming to life with a new energy and creativity? And as I catch myself asking these questions, I notice that the context of my questioning is narrowing by the minute. The room is becoming a more and more confined space as the agenda shrinks down to him and me and my task to help him discover a spirituality to give a greater wholeness to his life. I notice also the range of my interests and the breadth of my commitment decreasing, as he becomes individuated before me, set apart from the world in which we both live, concerned more and more with his life and his God. The conversation does not, in content, resemble an old-fashioned self-examination, but the feeling it induces is strangely similar to the one induced by those self-examinations I have made and heard where life is reduced to a series of minor incidents which might with profit have been handled differently — although it would not have made much difference if they had been. There is the same sense of a scratching where it does not really itch, but where, we have both of us been told, perhaps it ought to and where, if we scratch hard enough, perhaps it will.

There is the possibility that really attentive listening will offer some clues or alternatively give Philip that affirmation that will enable him to find his own clues, enter more fully into his own distress and find his own way through. There is also a chance that if I knew my ascetic theology rather better I might have some useful advice to offer that will break the cycles of repetition and detachment. My mind rebels against both these possibilities into a series of quite different questions, questions that seek somehow if they can to break down the narrow confines of the room.

For is there not an immense luxury about the pursuit of this small agenda, particularly when you contrast the content of the items with the grand names by which they are called? Words such as God, prayer, faith — these hardly match the sense of vague interest — or is it lack of it, it is hard to tell? — that pervades the conversation. Are not the times too urgent and the days too critical to allow for such hobbies to be so pretentiously described? Is there not a world out there beyond the tightly shut door? And is God really so absent from its triumphs and its sufferings as to need to be provided with space in this small room? And is there the slightest hope that Philip will break out of a seemingly dilettante interest in himself without there coming into the room, somehow, that larger drama going on in the world outside which might give to our small joint enterprise a seriousness appropriate to what it claims as its purpose?

There is indeed an issue between the values traditionally associated with Christianity and the values that have come from the world of counselling and therapy. There is the question whether we should consider human beings as primarily fallen or primarily beautiful and good. Yet this issue is placed in a new perspective by my encounter with Philip. We seem to be lacking any larger context of the world outside, any sense of the purpose his gifts might be fulfilling or which his failures might be frustrating. So the question of his beauty or his fallenness is arising, as it were, in a vacuum. He is there without his history and without the history of those with whom he is in contact. This is spiritual direction outside the real world and therefore outside the arena in which God's faithfulness is active and is also being put to the test.

Jane comes to see me for the same reason. She too wishes to examine her own life of prayer. She is older and has done community work for some years. But if her agenda is similar to Philip's, the atmosphere of our conversation is entirely different.

There is here no want of seriousness, for all talk is in the context of the possibility that a life which many have affirmed to have been valuable should turn out to have been for nothing in the eyes of a God who is felt to be totally demanding of her life and her allegiance. There is no absence here of the light and shade of the real world. The talk is dominated by a kind of holy fear that moves very close at times to being an unholy one as a very fragile self-esteem comes near to breaking point. There must be some way, I have often said to myself, to ease that terrible burden and to make possible a confident and entirely appropriate appreciation of all that has been accomplished and of the love — of God and of other people — in which she is held. But then, I ask myself, for whom would this greater tranquillity of spirit be a benefit? Certainly it would be a benefit to me; for such real self-doubt rings too many bells as you listen to it and the conversation would be very much easier if you did not have to. It is just possible it might be a benefit for her, although the dynamic of dealing with that self-doubt has been so strong a force in her life that to take it away might well be to take away too much. Maybe staying present with that dynamic, offering solidarity with that loneliness without seeking to take it away, a sign perhaps of a God who not for the first time is really absent, and present in the absence, is a more creative offering. Creative, that is, for those who still need her commitment. That commitment is required by God also. In that larger context, of a world of suffering and a God who cares for it, it may be more important to affirm as beautiful a person's own sense of fallenness in the face of the demands of the time as she sees them, rather than to seek in the name of beauty to take the sense of fallenness away.

Jane reminds me of another person whom I watched with increasing alarm. John was involved in political campaigning with a fragile energy that resisted all attempts to minister to him until the collapse or near-collapse of his interior landscape made a concern with his own inner self unavoidable and revealed the insecurity of his previous engagement with the life of the world outside and how foolish it would have been for others to rely on it. Any attempt to minister to John by giving to him the attention and affirmation he clearly needed had to accept his engagement with the world as a vital reality, and not to assume it had been an escape. In part it may have been an escape, but the world remains the inescapable context in which we seek any personal wholeness and it is for the Christian the place of vocation. I recall well having been at the point John is at, and the one thing that again and again caused me to resist any attempts at ministering to me was a fear, often at a rational level groundless, but very strong nevertheless, that under the impact of all that love that was on offer, the world out there and the God whom I know to be longing for its wholeness might be made to seem unimportant.

Christianity's traditional view of people as fallen creatures and the insistence by the practitioners of the modern arts of mental healing on our intrinsic beauty and resourcefulness seem therefore to be neither in simple agreement nor simply opposed. Both direct us to more majestic possibilities in living. We lose those possibilities if we see our beauty or our fallenness as opposed to one another. Beauty and fallenness are seen only against a background, and that background is the wider world for whose wholeness we are responsible. Both require us to take seriously the context which is affecting our quest for wholeness. If we ignore that context, true beauty is replaced by a false pleasantness and true fallenness by lesser stumblings. Too narrow and too private a perspective makes human living lose both its grandeur and its tragedy.

The human potential movement was not only a revolt against religion's tendency to reduce and demean people by what it said about personhood; it sought to question also the rigid classification of experiences into 'sick' and 'healthy' that had arisen from the application of medical categories to what have become known as mental illnesses or disorders. In fact, our coming of age in the world of our feelings has the treatment of the mentally ill as one very important impetus in its history. When the mentally ill ceased to be contained for protection and custody in asylums and were moved into the setting of a hospital for something called treatment, it was inevitable that a medical model of mental illness should come to prevail — and in a whole host of situations that model was seen to work. People got better. In that context psychotherapy, which is in reality a rather special kind of conversation, came to be understood, like electroconvulsive therapy or drugs, as a matter of dosage; that is to say, the application of some remedy from the outside of a person in an attempt to heal the disorder. In fact, psychotherapy opens up areas of personal experience hidden no less from the healthy than from the ill — indeed, often rather more hidden from the healthy than from the ill — and therefore places a very large question mark against any categorization of experiences as normal or abnormal. Such categorization is a political act, a determination by society of what is to count as 'normal' and therefore tolerable; and as R. D. Laing points out, there is a high level of alienation from experience present in behaviour that is classified by society as entirely normal.

> There are forms of alienation that are relatively strange to statistically 'normal' forms of alienation. The 'normally' alienated person, by reason of the fact that he acts more or less like everyone else, is taken to be sane. Other forms of alienation that are out of step with the prevailing state of

alienation are those that are labelled by the 'normal' majority as bad or mad.

The condition of alienation, of being asleep, of being unconscious, of being out of one's mind, is the condition of the normal man.

Society highly values its normal man. It educates children to lose themselves and to become absurd, and thus to be normal.

Normal men have killed perhaps a million of their fellow normal men in the past fifty years.[4]

Laing's trenchant demonstrations of the craziness of the normal and the wisdom of the abnormal is a clear expression of the desire, also present in much of the human potential movement, to free us from medical models of mental health and illness and to invite us all into an exploration of levels of experience which lie below the level of our conscious, censored lives. The experiences of those called psychotic provide access to levels of reality which 'normal' people have learned to conceal from themselves, and those same normal people can, by bringing experience which is half-hidden from them in the background of their lives into the foreground (a major aim of Gestalt therapy), give themselves access to a far fuller range of experience.

Both religion and therapy therefore have it in them to provide access to some of the majesty of human experience and both are capable of trivialization. The experience of therapy is trivialized when it is simply gained and possessed without being allowed to give access to the fullness of a person's context, the extent to which they have been alienated from their own feelings and inner world, and the way in which that has happened. Religion is trivialized when too narrow a perspective transforms the full challenge of a God who calls us to engagement with the fullness of the human situation into a narrowly individualistic moralism.

So all pastoral care, all concern with spirituality and human growth has to take account of the location of individuals in their context in society. The human potential movement and the churches share with each other a certain middle-class captivity, and that is not surprising. For it is middle-class people who are least likely to feel the need to locate themselves politically because they like to think of themselves as in the middle and for that reason to have transcended the status of a vested interest. It is they who are most likely to reduce human potential to narcissistic self-indulgence and a religious view of the meaning of persons to a matter of small virtues and small shortcomings. A spiritual or psychological practice that does not seek to locate its participants in relation to the perpetrators of oppression in the world outside and to its victims has no contribution to make to the realization of human potential, let alone to the encounter of the person with the God whose commitment is to the struggle for justice, freedom and peace.

Our feelings, our inner world, give us a way into a knowledge of where we stand in relation to the larger drama going on in the world outside. To take the examples mentioned earlier, Philip's attitude expressed very clearly his remoteness from any issues outside himself, while Jane's fear that her life might have been a waste is a very clear demonstration of what a person is given to feel whose life is expended for the dispensable and unwanted members of society. To deal with individual experience as though it were simply the private property of the individual who is having it is to reduce it to insignificance, and that is just as true whether the experience is being handled from the standpoint of humanistic psychology or religious belief. We neutralize the efficacy of our pastoral care by using it as a means of isolating people from the question of where they stand in the dramas of oppression and liberation, of peacemaking or warmongering in the world outside.

Yet, as I have indicated, our most intimate encounters can make it possible for us to locate ourselves and those with whom we are in contact in relation to the wider world. We pastor one another, and we learn to pray not only in relation to those inner and individual dramas of which the advance of the human sciences seems to require us to take charge. We pastor one another, and we learn to pray in relation to the drama of human history which determines so much of what we individually experience. To know that may give us insights we can share with those with whom we are pastorally engaged and thereby bring about their healing. It may enable us to help people to have higher expectations of themselves, to know that the world is something which they are not simply to fit into but also sometimes to seek to change. To know that may also teach us something of the very real vested interest we have in the exercise of the pastoral role and the way in which the healing of individuals may actually leave the cause of their hurt untouched. We may also be enabled to revise what is very often a far too simple view of human suffering: the view that suffering is simply human, something individuals experience because they are human and not somehow related to their location within the pressures and conflicts of society at large.

There is, for example, an overwhelming difference in the suffering of the poor on the one hand and that of the rich who have been sent empty away, and to describe the experience of both as alienation, or suffering, or neurosis, or fallenness or sin is to run the risk of obscuring the distinction and therefore maintaining the situation as it is. It is, for instance, clearly true that the white people of the world have caused themselves to suffer immense personal and cultural loss by their domination over, and therefore their isolation from, black people. It is also true that they need to overcome some of that loss if they are ever going to be able to desist from their racism. What is a gross distortion is to say that white people and black people are all harmed as a result of racism and that all need liberating from it. That would be to suggest that the black experience of white racism is the same as the white experience of it, and for any white person to suggest that is to deny responsibility.

Or again, any group of men who seek to make an adequate response to the movement for the liberation of women need to look at the interior disturbance which they suffer as a result of their socialization as men in a male-dominated world and the even greater disturbance which arises when that world starts to change. That process, though painful, can also be highly rewarding as men come to discard some very destructive patterns and find a new freedom, so much so that it is then easy to forget that the object of the exercise was to interrupt the pattern of oppressing women. They may even start talking about the liberation of men. Before we know where we are, we are into mischievous talk about how we are all in the same boat — which we cannot be, otherwise there would not be a problem; the fact is that some people are in the boat and others are not!

It is entirely possible for the middle-class Christian or humanist to ignore this very uncomfortable issue, and actually to seek to minimize disturbance which really needs to be experienced and faced. Instead, to use a biblical image that makes the point very well, we set up processes designed to remove the maggots from manna that has been gathered to excess and stored for too long. Most of us have in one context or another made some peace with the world's oppression, and much of our suffering is the dis-ease that results from that. Whatever pastoral care is, it is surely not a device for interfering with what Christians are bound to identify as part of the divinely instituted process of judgement; and whatever prayer is, it surely cannot be a series of procedures for insulating the soul from an unease we have every reason to feel. And if the human potential movement has potential only for those humans who engage in it, it were better it did not exist.

It is worth noticing, in conclusion, that using pastoral encounters to locate people within the much larger drama of human history and the purpose of God is nothing especially new, nor is it something that has simply arisen out of recent developments in the field of pastoral care, counselling and human growth movements. One very traditional arena in which individuals gave and received pastoral help and spiritual direction was that of sacramental confession. In modern terms the practice may seem lacking in flexibility, spontaneity and mutuality. It may appear all too much like a very hierarchical way of giving and receiving help. One person sits while the other kneels. The counsel that is given is frequently highly directive and there is often an emphasis on the breaking and keeping of rules.

Yet to make these points is to judge the practice of confession by the standards of modern counselling practice. The assumptions behind confession are fundamentally different. They are that human weakness, failure and distress are not simply the occasion for assistance to be sought; they are occasions for worship. They are, that is to say, no less than the obviously good things of life, to be celebrated and offered to the One who has a good purpose for the creation and, more than that, will gather up all things into that purpose. What is going on is not the wiping clean of a slate so that the individual leaves with a blank where previously there were sins. The purpose of confession and absolution is a proclamation that people leave with what they brought, but what they brought has been made an occasion of freedom (absolution) instead of an occasion of bondage. What presented itself to them as weakness, sin and shortcoming is instead to be built into the fabric of the reign of God; what was bad is actually made to be good; what was nothing is made into something just as it was in the beginning of the universe.

Thus a proclamation is made, the more important precisely because its context begins as the experience of human failure, that the whole of existence, no less what we call bad than what we call good, finds its significance in the presence and purpose of God. Whether I feel better for knowing that or not is significant, but it is not the most significant thing. The most significant thing is that as a matter of fact the whole of my personal history and that of the society of which I am a part can find renewed significance.

Our coming of age in relation to our inner life and our feelings has made all sorts of developments possible in the field of pastoral care. What it also makes possible, and important, is the relating of that inner world which has become so significant to us, to the external world of which we are also together in charge. We are accountable for what we do with our understanding of human feelings and inner experiences. They are signals of where we stand personally in the world's struggle for wholeness. It is part of spiritual awareness to notice those signals and part of pastoral care to enable that noticing to happen. Then we can be alert to the way in which our own quest for human meaning is also a window into the world's superhuman struggle for life.

FIVE

Our Own Work

Considering how hard it is for many of us to delegate, it is in fact remarkably easy to get other people to do our work for us by projection. Delegation and projection are of course very different from each other. The process of delegation is a conscious one, involving the assent of two parties, the one delegating and the one taking up the responsibility. It involves therefore a conscious process of letting go of some piece of work and trusting that the person taking it up will do the job adequately, and for the recipient of the task it means the willingness to take on something new and extra. The other process to which I refer, getting someone to do our work for us by projection, is quite different. It is a process that is unconscious, one in which neither party has much idea what is going on, although both may in different ways have a sense that something rather strange is happening. Somebody becomes very angry or very sad, and senses that the source of that anger or sadness is something they do not completely understand. There may even be a sense that the emotion does not really belong to them.

This happening is most clearly observable in the life of small groups set up for the express purpose of learning about the life of the group itself; but it is discernible in all kinds of groups. Groups of people are not just aggregates of individuals; they constitute systems with their own identity and their own capacity to affect the individuals who make them up. Energy of any kind, be it happiness, anger, frustration or whatever, seeks a place to manifest itself, and when it manifests itself it diverts attention from its real source.

You are at a committee meeting. You have not felt particularly involved, but the meeting has gone on rather a long time. Suddenly you look across the room and see somebody yawning. Seeing the yawn makes you realize that you are bored. You start shuffling papers, and in the process catch somebody else's eye. They too have realized that they are bored. The boredom that led to one person's yawn was not created by the yawn; it was there all the time, the property of the whole meeting, shared in to varying degrees by those present. Maybe most of them were too polite to show it, and the person who did show it was slightly less polite and therefore allowed the yawn to come. Maybe that person was overtired, and so became the ideal person to express the boredom that was in the room. Perhaps everybody else would have denied that they were bored if they had been asked point blank, but the expression of the feeling by one person present enables the total situation to be recognized.

You are at church with your children, and they start to become extremely fractious. You are cross with them and attempt to restore order. As often happens, you are more successful at getting cross than at restoring order. On your way home you reflect that it was a rather awful occasion and you wish you had not had to be there. Did all the fractiousness belong to the children or were they simply expressing on behalf of your family (and, for that matter, others too) the irritation present in the congregation so that the blame that was levelled at them was levelled at them unfairly?

Or you visit friends and during the course of the evening one of the friends breaks down and weeps uncontrollably. You spend the evening counselling and consoling that friend, and it is not until some days later that you realize that you too feel a great sadness, not occasioned by the weeping of your friend but by something in your own life. It was in the back of your mind when you went on that visit, but you put it out of your mind and were not particularly thinking about it. The weeping was your weeping too.

So projection happens. It has been observed time and again in small groups and in families and organizations. From time to time, however, it manifests itself in a far less savoury way, in groups where individuals behave in ways that are deeply distressing and which nobody concerned understands while it is happening. Mr and Mrs Edwards, a very well respected couple whose advice was much sought after, were pillars of the local community. They seemed to give their children an enormous amount. Then they found that their middle child, Brian, had started to behave in a highly disturbed way. Eventually he dropped out of school, and finally came up before the magistrates. The parents were deeply perplexed and very angry with the child concerned, and in their distress they found themselves looked upon no longer with respect but more with pity in the community at large. Then it emerged, as people began to inquire into what had happened, that all in the past was not as it had appeared, that the relationship between the parents was not quite as harmonious as their public face had previously suggested, and that in the community there were considerable feelings of jealousy about the reputation in which this family stood. Brian's behaviour was only partly, it seemed, the result of his disturbance, and if others in the family could in the past have been more open about their negative feelings, Brian might not have had to act out as much; similarly, if the community had not seen fit to maintain its solid front of respect for a family about which some people in fact had had considerable doubts, then some of the difficulty might have been averted. The damage done to individuals who bear more than their appropriate share of negative feelings can be very great.

There can be no denying that the opposite also happens, and we blame others for feelings which actually have their origin inside ourselves. Paranoia is probably the best known example of that, where a strongly aggressive and angry person is convinced that all anger and aggression are outside them, being directed at them by others. Betty has told me many times how her house is bugged and how people sneak into it (although it is locked) and read her private letters. It is noticeable that she is constantly spying on her neighbours and forming violently negative judgements about them. But that fact about herself she cannot face — and so she blames her neighbours for all the spying and backbiting that goes on. Unlike the Edwards family, where Brian expresses all the badness, Betty constructs for herself a world that is wholly bad so that she will not need to accept that any of the badness belongs to her. She lives in danger of her fantasies building up to such a point that normal life will become impossible.

The mechanism whereby we get others to do our work for us can be highly pernicious as we make unconscious deals

with one another. Betty builds up her world around the idea
that we are persecuting her; we build up ours around the
belief that she is deluded. Our belief that she is deluded
convinces her that we are persecuting her, and so the spiral
twists on. The feelings of anger roam around, seeking a
person to consume, and when the burden finally lands it does
so with all the energy of those who have yet to admit that any
of the anger belongs to them.

Such is the degree to which we are tied to one another that
almost every feeling we have or action we take is the result of
some sort of deal made between factors inside ourselves and
things that are given to us by people outside ourselves. The
anger or the sadness or the boredom does not all belong to the
'other people' who are not acknowledging or expressing it.
Nor, on the other hand, does it all belong to me as an isolated
individual. My feelings and my behaviour are the result of
some inner encounter between me and the world around me,
so that in part I do for others what they are unwilling to do
for themselves and they do for me in return much of what I
am unwilling to do for myself. This close intertwining of
human lives is most beautifully expressed by Kahil Gibran
when the prophet is asked to speak about crime and
punishment:

> Oftentimes have I heard you speak of those who commit a
> wrong as though they were not part of you, but strangers
> unto you and intruders upon your world.

> But I say that even as the holy and the righteous cannot
> rise beyond the highest which is in each one of you,

> So the wicked and the weak cannot fall lower than the
> lowest which is in you also.

> And as a single leaf turns not yellow but with the silent
> knowledge of the whole tree,

> So the wrongdoer cannot do wrong without the hidden will
> of you all.[1]

So human beings act in hidden concert with each other.
Because we are part of one another and have the capacity to
get others to do our work there is no event for which we are
not included in the chain of responsibility. Even those who in

any particular case turn out to be victims are participators in that social energy that leads to their misfortune.

And this also, though the word lie heavy upon your hearts:

The murderer is not unaccountable for his own murder.

And the robber is not blameless in being robbed.

The righteous is not innocent of the deeds of the wicked,

And the white-handed is not clean in the doings of the felon.

Yea, the guilty is oftentimes the victim of the injured.

And still more often the condemned is the burden bearer for the guiltless and the unblamed.

You cannot separate the just from the unjust and the good from the wicked;

For they stand together before the face of the sun even as the black thread and the white are woven together.

And when the black thread breaks, the weaver shall look into the whole cloth, and he shall examine the loom also.

If any of you would bring to judgement the unfaithful wife,

Let him also weigh the heart of her husband in scales and measure his soul with measurements.

And let him who would lash the offender look unto the spirit of the offended.

And if any of you would punish in the name of righteousness and lay the axe unto the evil tree, let him see to its roots;

And verily he will find the roots of the good and the bad, the fruitful and the fruitless, all entwined together in the silent heart of the earth.[2]

This statement about the intertwined nature of the human community can of course be reduced to absurdity if it is taken to mean that we are all equally and in the same way responsible for every wrongdoing. We do not become accomplices in the burglary of our houses by choosing to go out for the evening. We do, however, share with the burglar in the culture of acquisition and in a society where to possess is to be valued. The burglary is one crop that grows from soil in which the roots of the burglar and the law-abiding are intertwined.

What we encounter when we concern ourselves with spirituality or the care of others is never the isolated experience of individuals. Taking responsibility for our lives means taking responsibility for that intertwining. In that regard too we are come of age. We have to accept accountability for our life together as families, groups and communities and for the forces which operate within them, for these too are no longer matters of totally uncharted mystery in which we can do no more than accept what takes place as inevitable. The possibility of our assuming adult responsibility for our life together and the forces which operate within it is signalled by the growth of knowledge about the dynamics of groups and organizations.

That possibility also shows in the amount of work being done in the treatment of whole families whose members, or some of them, may be showing signs of disturbed and disturbing behaviour. Casework agencies have found by repeated experience that handling all problems as though they were the property of the person presenting them simply does not work. Similarly, there has been much growth in the work being done with communities and neighbourhoods as such for the creation of more humane attitudes and a more creative environment for all those who make up that community. We now know that to attend only to the needs of individuals who are distressed or who need help of one kind or another, as has been the tradition of some casework, is often to ignore fundamental causes of distress within a community, and by ignoring them to ensure that they remain unremedied.

This has major implications for the Christian churches. They, after all, offer care to their own members and to the community at large. They are concerned for the spiritual formation of those who seek to deepen their life of faith. The fact is that even for those who profess most strongly the individual nature of the Christian life and the personal nature of the relationship we have with God, formation in discipleship is a corporate matter. The shape of faith, whatever may be done about it privately in the silence of a person's own room, is overwhelmingly determined by the common life of Christians and its liturgical and pastoral character.

The effect on individuals of altering the nature of the life of the Christian community or altering its liturgy may not be immediate, but it is sure. That is hardly surprising. Believers grow up and are formed by the experience of congregational life. The pattern of authority which a clergyman exercises is not just an organizational or constitutional matter. It is a pattern of authority which grew up because it was felt to be appropriate to the pattern of rule God exercises in the world. The style of fellowship which a congregation experiences in its life together impresses itself on members as a model of what fellowship we are *meant* to have with each other.

When we hear in liturgy or preaching the great themes of the gospel referred to, the words reverberate with all our past experience of common discipleship in the Church. If you seek to change a liturgy or propose some new pattern of life together in a church, you disturb not merely the words or the patterns you seek to change but the whole intertwining of the roots of people — and that may only become clear when you do disturb it. If, furthermore, you speak to people of their Christian calling or their spiritual needs and how they are to be met, you stir up echoes of a corporate experience and an organizational pattern. We may want to distinguish in theory between the authority of the clergy and the authority of God — but the distinction has to fight against a tradition which will have caused the former to model the latter.

So also a congregation expresses something of the nature of the community in which it is set. A place which is hard to live in and where people have difficulty in surviving will generate a congregation to do its work of creating a place of belonging; the congregation in such a place is often small and intimate — but also not easy to join if you are an outsider. Congregation and community are bound together in a network and pattern of relationships which critically affect how pastoral care is offered and spirituality fostered.

It belongs to the nature of coming of age that we make ourselves aware of the ways in which we are getting other people to do our feeling and our acting for us on the basis that that will enable us to choose to take responsibility for our own feeling and acting. Any capacity we might have to put ourselves in relationship to Christ in a world come of age, to undertake, that is, a spirituality for our times, and through our pastoral care to enable other people to do so, will involve taking responsibility for our personal share, our congregation's share and our community's share, of what is going on.

We can still as come-of-age adults allow space for passivity and dependence; but our passivity and dependence are to be chosen. They are not postures we adopt out of an unchecked assumption that they are the only possible postures we can adopt. If I freely place myself in dependence on somebody, that does not impose upon them the duty to make up for my passivity by their activity and to take responsibility for my weakness: they are to have the same freedom that I have. And if we are to speak of knowing Christ in a world come of age, then that mutual freedom has also to apply to the posture we take in relation to God. The reality is not that we are empty vessels until God fills us up, powerless creatures until God empowers us; we are summoned to a relationship of the free co-operation of independent partners, to do our own work that God might be able to do God's. There is in that relationship the possibility of dependence, but that dependence is not there as a prior requirement laid on people so that they never grow up.

> And we cannot be honest unless we recognize that we have to live in the world *etsi deus non daretur*. And this is just what we do recognize — before God! God himself compels us to recognize it. So our coming of age leads us to a true recognition of our situation before God. God would have us know that we must live as men who manage our lives without him. The God who is with us is the God who forsakes us (Mark 15.34). The God who lets us live in the world without the working hypothesis of God is the God before whom we stand continually. Before God and with God we live without God.[3]

These words are reminiscent of the rabbi's response to the question, why was atheism created? — 'so that we should not rely on God when we work in the world, but carry on as if

God did not exist, and the responsibility was ours alone'.[4] If there is to be dependence it can be in either direction:

Men go to God when they are sore bestead,
Pray to him for succour, for his peace, for bread,
For mercy for them sick, sinning, or dead;
All men do so, Christian and unbelieving.

Men go to God when he is sore bestead,
Find him poor and scorned, without shelter or bread,
Whelmed under weight of the wicked, the weak, the dead;
Christians stand by God in his hour of grieving.

God goes to every man when sore bestead,
Feeds body and spirit with his bread;
For Christians, pagans alike he hangs dead,
And both alike forgiving.[5]

This paragraph and this poem of Bonhoeffer's are famous enough, and have constituted a major arena of theological debate. Is there not some inescapable sense in which our relationship with God cannot be mutual if God is to be God? If there is a sense in which God can become dependent on us, is that dependence different in kind from any dependence we might have on God? Is not God's dependence on us a condescension, a chosen weakness in a way ours cannot be? The speed with which some have rushed to detect in Bonhoeffer's words more than the first signs of pride, and to defend the unique Godness of God, does not leave me with much confidence that they have faced with full seriousness the experience of which Bonhoeffer was speaking, or the experience that is available to us when we embark on the road of taking full responsibility for our part in the life of the world.

A key way in which that experience is becoming available in society and in the Church is through our rising concern with the question of leadership and the debate about the question of authority. The fact is that the experiences of a lifetime in being on the receiving end of parenting, teaching, governing, pastoring provide the unspoken parameters within which any images we might have of God as Lord, Father, King, Shepherd are built up. Any changes in those patterns of leadership are bound to be experienced over time as altering our fundamental perception of reality as containing an inescapable element of hierarchy; and hierarchy in that context is understood in a systematic ordering of things such that leaders can share fully the lives of followers but only leaders can share fully in the work and concerns of leaders. That is why experiments with shared leadership have not, where they have been tried seriously, been found to be a gentle process of delegation, involving the setting up of a few new committees with wider representation or the sharing out of some of the pastor's jobs. Both may happen, but they are not the point.

The central point has to do with coming of age, in the very precise sense of bringing to an end the state of affairs in which it is possible to locate responsibility for one's experience and one's action, whether as a citizen or as a member of a congregation, in the all-powerful machinations of some 'them' or other. Such a movement of the spirit of a community cannot but affect how it sees itself as standing in relationship to its God, and the tenacious way in which some communities resist the movement towards responsibility suggests that they know the ultimate significance of that movement only too well. It is not a palatable thought that the constantly reiterated biblical message of human responsibility for the created universe might finally turn out to be true.

If human responsibility for the world is a reality, then our conception of God changes in the process. The all-powerful God who takes all the credit and all the blame does not simply turn into one who is willing to leave some of the more routine jobs for human beings to do — like some managing director who has learned the art of delegation. God becomes one whose own destiny as well as ours is tied up with the choices we have to make; there is now no point of last resort. God's supreme vulnerability is indeed shown in a historical crucifixion in which we were allowed to do what we willed with the one called Master and Lord; and that vulnerability might extend to permitting the divine authority to be flouted to the end. That perception places us spiritually in an entirely new arena from which we understandably seek to escape if we can. That arena is one in which the will of the Creator and the will of the creature have to find a way of co-operation and exchange; and we find it even more daunting as an arena when we reflect that in a nuclear age the consequences of not finding a way are disastrous.

The struggles over leadership and how it is to be exercised in the small congregations and communities to which we belong are not just an interesting hobby for those who find group dynamics a stimulating exercise but a very valuable resource in spirituality and in our caring for people. To notice the tensions and the creative excitement that arise under the impact of changing patterns of authority and leadership is to notice something which has the possibility of presenting before our very eyes both the cost and the potential creativity of responsible living, and life with God, in a world come of age. W. R. Bion's account of the work which groups do about their basic assumptions even as they are engaged in whatever their task happens to be[6] revolves almost completely around the issue of leadership, the kind of work the group wishes the leader to do for it and the possibility, always elusive, that the group might come to be able to do that work for itself. So powerful are the basic assumptions present in the group about the kind of things it expects from its leaders, and so strong are the feelings which the group projects into them that in Bion's view what the leader is experiencing and feeling at any given moment is sufficient basis for an interpretation of what is going on in the group.

In his description of the way in which any group has to engage with its basic assumptions, he paints a highly suggestive picture of groups as places where we have to enter into a replay of our most powerful, earliest and most fundamental experiences in living. We experience some of the tension we felt as children in our relationship to our parents, both wanting and not wanting what they have to offer, both striving after and rejecting the emerging possibility of independence, a possibility in which sometimes we believe and sometimes we do not. Not only does that description conjure up echoes of countless struggles in the lives of groups, congregations and communities; it also reminds us of our encounters with a God whom we at one and the same time seek to dethrone and demand to be behind everything.

What goes on in groups and communities, however, reminds us of more than our childhood experiences and the way they reflect our encounter with God. We also experience something much more akin to the adolescent ambivalence about belonging. 'Shall I stay at home or go off and have a flat of my own?' is the symbolic question that expresses the situation of someone on the verge of being of age, with all its profound uncertainty about whether we need to belong or can manage on our own or, put another way, whether in belonging we can find any independence or not. That struggle is mirrored in groups by the tension between centrifugal and centripetal forces, those which tend to hold the group together and those which tend to make it fly apart. The role of those who do not turn up for meetings, for example, is that although those who do come resent them, the absent do in fact in their absence represent the doubt in the group about whether staying together will achieve anything and whether it is all worth the toil and trouble of attempting to co-operate with other people. Equally, those who are not there may well express resentment about those who did attend and, for instance, make some decisions, and who represent the need of the group, both absent and present members, to be kept in being.

If we split the functions of expressing the desire to belong and the desire for independence in that unacknowledged way we are not taking on responsibility in the group as a whole for both desires; instead we set up a conflict in which one set of feelings is designated as good and the other bad. In reality it is the tension between the two which is what prevents the group from lapsing into total disintegration on the one hand, if the centrifugal force prevails utterly, or totalitarian domination of the individual members on the other, if the centripetal force is entirely victorious.

Once again group life conjures up echoes of some of the basic conflicts of individual life. It also has profound implications for a spirituality for a world that is of age. One of the demands that a group certainly makes of its leader is to be a focus of unity, to formulate consensus and thus to be the expression of policies which will bring about a common mind in the group. The leader is supposed not to take sides when the group splits into factions but to seek to find a basis for coming together. The leader is certainly supposed to be far more interested in sustaining the centripetal force, the one that holds the group together, than in the centrifugal force which is seen as the one most threatening to its survival. Yet in a world that has very good reason for being desperately concerned for peace and unity, and in a Church with some great anxieties about its own survival, it is crucial though difficult that we accept responsibility for our desire for both independence and belonging.

The Church's own tradition contains enough of a basis for taking both desires seriously. It is a corporate tradition, the tradition of a people, called together into one and sustaining a common life of worship and discipleship. It is the story of a people among whom God's dwelling has been made and belonging to that people is part of what is involved in belonging to God. At the same time the very identity of that people is as a collection of those who remember that their background is the background of outsiders. 'Remember that you were slaves in Egypt.' 'You were sinners, cut off from the life of God.' It is a Hebrew people, an outsider people; it is the people in whose governing teaching there appears a treasury of stories with that fundamental message: the lost coin, the lost sheep, the labourers in the vineyard. Their master was crucified outside the gate, and Paul, the apostle who most conditioned the Church's formative theological outlook, set his face towards the Gentile mission. If natural human communities find their belonging very often in excluding outsiders, the gospel is clear that real belonging depends upon a recognition that the God who calls us into belonging is also the one who is found among the lost and the outcast. Holding these strands together against our fear of disintegration is one difficulty. Holding them together against our fear of excessive closeness is another.

The difficulty which community membership has in owning its own desire for freedom, to cut loose and find its independence leads to a constant domestication, a making homely, of the drama to which the faith bears witness. Meanwhile, those on the fringe and beyond the edge of the Christian community sense that they are left alone and God-forsaken because to rejoin seems to mean the total loss of independence and a surrender to a totalitarian, centripetal force in which they feel they have no part. Those who would see themselves as belonging and those who see themselves as having opted for freedom carry out an unacknowledged division of labour, and no progress is made towards a kind of belonging which leaves people's freedom intact or a kind of freedom which does not leave us feeling isolated and alone. Central to our coming of age, then, is our responsibility as communities and as individuals for both apartness and togetherness. We have to stop demanding of parents or leaders or priests or of our God that we should be allowed to shelve the responsibility that is in reality ours. We have to create a freedom in belonging and a solidarity in freedom that the human spirit needs. There is nobody who can do that task for us. The requirement that parents should be at home, our leaders in the office, and our priests in the church, and that they should be there *for us* is a refusal of responsibility for deciding our own relationship to the issue of freedom and belonging. Its spiritual counterpart is the demand that God should always be at the centre, holding things together, so that we know where God can be found.

To accept the reality of our coming of age is to enter again and again into the reality of our inheritance of responsibility. It involves ceasing to project that responsibility outward. The process of taking back into ourselves the responsibilities we have sought to get other people to carry, and particularly our responsibility for those feelings and attitudes which we believe to be bad, is seldom carried out without considerable pain. Often it only happens when those on whom the responsibility has been projected find a way of refusing to carry it any more. For their pains they encounter a great deal of hostility. But this is a matter of a far more profound urgency than can be appreciated if we think that it has to do with the domestic life of small communities or congregations or the interesting hobby of learning about how groups work. There is very much more to play for in trying to come to the point where we take responsibility for our own attitudes and feelings instead of asking somebody else to express them for us.

We have become accustomed to identifying certain groups and asking them to be the bearers of part of society's burden, so accustomed that we can hardly think of living any other way. If mental patients are in mental hospitals then we can see all our own emotional disturbance as located in them. That is not to say that there are not people who need to be in mental hospitals; only to make the point that far more are likely to be there than need to be because by being there they do something for the rest of us. If mental illness and emotional disturbance were something that we encountered far more frequently and inescapably every day in the community we might find it a great deal more difficult to suppose that disturbance was not part of the life of us all. There comes a stage, however, when the stresses in society reach a point where more and more people give way and hospital facilities are more and more under strain. Is it not important to ask, before that point is reached, whether something is going on for which we all have to take some responsibility?

As we watched crowds of young people, especially young black people, rioting in the centres of some of our cities, did we suppose that the heat of their anger was theirs alone? In a situation where the political process found no significant way of putting a brake on the persistent infliction of poverty and unemployment on young people in ever increasing numbers, given unions whose economic power had been sharply reduced in the recession, given the middle classes wringing their hands in impotent sympathy, where was the outrage supposed to go? Millions of us were also angry, also wished something could be done, but felt ourselves paralysed. What happens in such a situation is not that the anger disappears but that it surfaces with double force in a group that is convenient because it has little to lose and is already stereotyped as undisciplined and violent anyway. The process is bound to repeat itself until some means can be found for the political process to achieve what it is there to do, namely to take corporate responsibility for the ventilating and meeting of public grievances. That will involve the body politic, the citizens, those who claim to care about justice and even in some cases to care about justice in God's name, in ceasing to give to impersonal forces, recession, lack of competitiveness, inflation, the responsibility we in fact bear corporately for the priorities we set and the way in which we carry them out.

Pastoral care is very closely linked with the task of come-of-age human beings in assuming their shared responsibility and not passing it off on the most defenceless. To say that it is not, to say that it is confined to caring for individuals in isolation, is to evacuate the biblical imagery of shepherding of all its real significance. The shepherds of Israel are indeed required to build a community which does not purchase its life at the expense of the death or the exploitation of some of its members. Prayer and meditation, too, are not some species of personal hygiene by which individuals isolate themselves from anything that might ruffle the still waters of their inner tranquillity. It involves undertaking that inner struggle which is our personal share of the search for wholeness in its corporate living by the community at large.

It is possible of course to deny, as many do, that human beings are intertwined in the way I have suggested. It can be denied that the phenomenon about which I have been speaking, that of getting other people to do our work for us by projection, really happens. No proof is possible, it may be claimed, that there is any connection between the absence of some people from a meeting of a group and the ambivalence of the membership, including those who do attend, about meeting at all. It is possible to deny that there is any sound reason for believing that those who engage in lawless behaviour are doing anything at all on behalf of those who are not. It is possible to maintain that social unrest of any kind is simply the result of the waywardness of the particular individuals who engage in it. The description of the rioting in the streets of our cities as 'pure greed' which has nothing whatever to do with unemployment, is a very good case in point. There are plenty who believe, and live by the belief, that human beings are in fact isolated individuals whose fate, whether they sink or swim, is their own responsibility and whose feelings and actions are just what they happen to choose. My experience is that those who hold that belief are either those who are not themselves bearing unduly heavy burdens or else they are those who, though bearing heavy burdens, accept the story that they are to blame and put up with their fate for fear of something far worse.

Whether we affirm or deny the power of the mechanisms of projection within the network of human relations will indeed depend on our individual experience, and specifically on the extent to which our experience has driven us to look again at the boundary between our world and the world outside; that means checking which of our beliefs and attitudes and feelings and actions come from us, for which we have to take responsibility and which we have no business putting on to others; and which come from others, in which case we have no responsibility except to refuse to do others' work for them. My own experience of that difficult process, one which included at various points care, therapy and spiritual counsel, has left me quite clearly of the opinion that those who bear the most burdens — of poverty, of blame, of everything — do so with the silent consent and sometimes even the militant approval of those whose real burdens they are. In that situation there can be no spirituality and there can be no adequate pastoral care that does not involve the adult task of assuming the burdens that are one's own; and to begin with that means noticing what those burdens are.

Two concluding examples will suffice to make the point, and they concern work and marriage. We seem to be engaged in the creation of two distinct categories of people, those who have work and whose work becomes increasingly demanding of skill, energy and time, and those who have no work, whose skills atrophy and who have immense amounts of time on their hands. The former are socially and economically rewarded, and the latter are punished. As routine employment becomes scarcer it will be increasingly difficult to be neutral between these two categories. Is it possible to believe that this development is simply the result of the aggregation of millions of individual preferences, and that therefore the solution lies in counselling the 'workaholic' towards a more balanced life and the workless out of their idleness?

The way things are, those with work are rewarded, both financially and in their status in the community, while those without work appear to be made to suffer. In the way in which the unemployed are spoken of, it is easy to detect that we justify that inequitable system of rewards by retaining the belief that the unemployed are somehow more idle than the rest of us. It is convenient to believe that there is a pool of idle people. But the leaf does not turn yellow without the silent knowledge of the whole tree. If we were to look at our attitudes more honestly, we might discover that work was not that popular after all. To create two nations in the way we seem to be doing is convenient for those of us who are working hard and holding on to what we have and are idle in the pursuit of change in a social order that is plainly destructive of human dignity and unjust in its allocation of resources. Whether we notice how our lives are intertwined with those of the unemployed will affect the pastoral care we offer. Either it will be geared simply to palliative measures that are the expression of concern for individuals or we shall be prepared to look at necessary social changes which are the only way in which real pastoral care can be offered.

The pastoral care which we give in connection with the marriage relationship clearly expresses the view that it is a matter for the couple somehow to manage. We can give counsel to prepare them and we can give counsel to help them to stay together or to separate. We can in short offer couples something to enable them to cope with what is in effect an immense personal challenge. On that understanding there are those who manage it and there are those who do not, and they may regard each other variously with envy, pity, sympathy, concern, admiration, respect, contempt or whatever. But the marriage that fails is not part of the marriage that succeeds; there is no connection, according to the way in which we offer care, between the success of marriage A and the failure of marriage B.

I find myself wondering how high the divorce rate needs to climb, and how many people need to reject the marriage institution altogether, before we start to suspect that we may have it wrong. Can it be that we are choosing to deal with the stability and instability, the constancy and inconstancy in all of us, and above all the combination of rigid refusal to change and massive perplexity in society at large, by creating two sorts of people, the stable, constant ones and the unstable, inconstant ones? We provide pastoral and spiritual resources to enable people to achieve membership in the former group, which further enhances the blameworthiness of those who still do not.

I find, broadly speaking, two attitudes being taken to the current difficulties facing the institution of marriage, a more conservative one and a more liberal one, and both attitudes seem to me immensely individualistic. The conservative assumption is that more people could succeed in sustaining their marriages if they tried harder and we should give them the kind of education and upbringing that would encourage them to do so. The liberal assumption is that we are fortunate to live in a world where there is far more freedom of choice about whether one stays married or not, that it is better to be in a situation where people are not compelled to stay together and that some rise in the divorce rate is bound to happen as the external constraints holding marriages together artificially, disappear.

As I speak with friends who have stayed married and friends who have not, I am certain that the situation is not like that at all. As to trying harder, many have tried very hard indeed to stay together and found with immense pain that they could not do so; and some have tried separating and found, however difficult their marriages were, that they could not manage the complete break. And as to the great freedom of choice which we are supposed to have as a result of the disappearance of many of the constraints holding marriages together artificially, my sense is that many who are staying together and many who have separated have not felt particularly free in doing so; they did and they do what they have to do because they can do no other.

What is wrong with the investment we make in marriage is not the format — the counselling, the liturgy — so much as the agenda. Our present agenda assumes that with the right interior resources, and these can be promoted if not supplied, individuals can do what is necessary to make a good marriage. In the light of that agenda the skills we bring to bear are personal counselling skills. But what about the things that unite those who stay together and those whose marriages come to break up? What about the double message which is being proclaimed all the time, on the one hand about the need for strong and stable family life, and on the other hand about the need for the kind of social mobility that will keep the economy working, but which removes people from the network of family relationships which made family life possible in previous generations?

If we were committed to taking adult responsibility together for the future of marriage, we should have to stop deciding in advance that it is the people who break up who have the problem; we should have to look instead at what are the constraints that make for stability or instability in all of us and what we are going to do about them. On that agenda there would be a long list of topics: the importance we attach to our career; the range of different kinds of relationship which we need and enjoy and their compatibility with marital faithfulness; the changing expectations of the place of women and men in society; the question of who bears ultimate responsibility for the rearing of children. Pursuing that agenda is not a substitute for the offering of assistance to particular individuals who may be asking for it in the interests of enabling their marriage to succeed if that is what they desire or to end if that is the choice they have made. But it is an extension of that individual concern into the world at large where the origins of many personal troubles lie.

These two issues, work and marriage, are high on the list of those who are involved in pastoral care at the present time. They relate to situations which are of very deep concern to people. They are issues where the wholeness of human life is at stake: they reveal the fact that the world does not divide between those who are managing their lives successfully and those who are not; because those who are not are often failing on behalf of those who seem to be managing. Perhaps, entwined in the inner heart of the earth, are the roots of us all. Life in a world come of age, then, consists in taking responsibility ourselves for what is our share and noticing that we are at the same time accepting from God what is now irrevocably humanity's share. We also see in the matters of work and marriage that the quest for human meaning is not, in the end, dealt with adequately by personal ministry to one another on its own. There also has to be the recognition that the world's superhuman struggle for justice and peace is manifested every time any one of us is threatened with meaninglessness. Life in a world come of age is life in superhuman struggle with the forces that threaten human meaning.

SIX

The Retreat to Biology

Your daily life is your temple and your religion.
Whenever you enter into it take with you your all.
Take the plough and the forge and the mallet and the lute,
The things you have fashioned in necessity or for delight.
For in reverie you cannot rise above your achievements nor fall lower than your failures.
And take with you all people:
For in adoration you cannot fly higher than their hopes nor humble yourself lower than their despair.[1]

If I seek any kind of encounter with God and suppose that I can set my mind free from the pressing issues which distress the world and distort the face of humanity, I make the spiritual journey into an exercise in tourism; it becomes a luxury cruise in which the life of the crew is of no account to me in comparison with the sun-drenched beaches and exotic places I have paid to go and see. For a time this will work, and indeed my cruise may pass uneventfully. But the time will come when the crew can bear it no longer and will find a way of pressing its claim for attention and fairness upon owners and passengers alike. Then I shall be stranded, strike-bound in some port, or find myself in the crossfire of some mutiny on the deck. There is no spiritual journey that does not take with extreme seriousness the interior and exterior events of my life, and those events locate me within the struggles of the human community. To presume to care for other human beings without taking into account the social and political causes of whatever distress they may be experiencing is to confirm them in their distress while pretending to offer healing.

To separate individuals from their environment, their spirit from their body and mind, their religion from their secularity and their personal from their public lives are forms of dualism. A Christian understanding of God's dealings with us rules out such a dualism. Even if it did not, dualism does not work even on its own terms. Our various experiences press against the dividing wall dualism seeks to construct; eventually the dividing wall caves in under the pressure. The crew will eventually mutiny. Truth will out, and the attempt to construct a world untroubled by the issues of our secular existence is bound to come to grief against the reality of the secular world which is the one we actually inhabit. Those who try, for example, to have a home life that is free from stress while pursuing a relentless ambition in their work, subjecting themselves to limitless strain, quickly find the stress carries over into the home. That is the dark side of the futility of dualism; we have to inhabit our public world as well as our private one. And, put positively, the Christian tradition bears witness to the fact that God also inhabits the public world — and that makes dualism unnecessary.

We have only just begun to discover the full dimensions and complexity of this interpenetration of our various kinds of experience. We are already clear that there is a close connection between the world of our feelings and emotions and the symptoms our body displays. The collapse of the old dualism of mind and body owes its origin in part to the fact that we now know that that dualism simply does not work. Handling bodies as though they were not endowed with minds is not effective; people just do not get better. So our observation has taught us the strength of the mind-body link, so that we no longer speak as though they were quite separate. But we have not always been so quick to stop separating the private world of the individual from the public world which is the source of many of the pressures that invade the private world.

The character of that invasion from the public world is immensely varied, and at the same time very powerful. There are direct and obvious links in the pollution of the environment; there are the social conditions under which people are compelled to live and which impose stresses beyond what it is reasonable to expect anyone to tolerate. Poverty, bad housing, insufficient educational opportunities and a high incidence of robbery and other violence against property or person are bound, whatever their direct physical effects, to load a person with mental stress which in turn is likely to manifest itself in physical symptoms.

There are, however, far less direct links. Some were indicated in Chapter 5. The capacity we have for getting others to do our work for us certainly includes the capacity to get others to feel for us, to be angry or sad for us, to be the unwilling and unknowing bearers of the burdens of our violence, jealousy or fear. To extend the ways of treating illness from one individualistic model, the physical, to another, the psychosomatic, is no gain if we fail to take seriously the way in which our lives are intertwined with each other. The causes of numerous diseases are not entirely known. We have to be aware of the contribution we may be making to the stress under which others may be living, and the marks of which they may be bearing in their bodies. Much talk of the psychosomatic roots of disease simply enhances the burden of responsibility borne by those who are already ill, so that in addition to whatever physical symptoms they may be suffering from they also have the sense that they may be responsible for them, without really knowing how.

The biblical traditions about healing show that our forebears were in no doubt about the social nature of disease. Many of those who at the present time claim to be promoting the practice of religious healing focus too much on the language and forms of the biblical stories without noticing their implications. The use of prayer and the laying on of hands and the call to the sick to have faith do indeed arise from a concern with the healing of the whole person. Yet often the sick person is individualized, taken out of context. The biblical healing narratives do precisely the opposite. Taken literally, the way in which sickness is often linked in the Bible with sin or attributed to the power of demons may be unacceptable. But behind that language is a profound appreciation that the sickness of any individual is but an instance, an example of the fundamental drama in which all human beings are involved.

The sick, therefore, are called upon to have faith. This is not some super-medicine, a plus factor, or an extra dimension that doctors do not know about. Faith is required because healing depends upon the belief that the deep dislocations in the life of the world, of which this particular sickness in this particular person is a sign and an instance, are being remedied by the presence and grace of God. That is why many of the stories about healing also contain a message for the healthy; their faith is also required, because they too are involved in the world's dislocation and incompleteness. 'Oftentimes I have heard you speak of one who commits a wrong as though he was not one of you', says Gibran's prophet; we easily take the same attitude to the sick and many of our treatments of them have that isolating effect. Yet the nature of much contemporary sickness, no less than the biblical traditions about healing, requires us to see just how social a phenomenon illness is.

The suggestion that illness has to be seen and dealt with as a communal phenomenon is on the face of it profoundly unattractive. Do not most of us want, and especially when we are at our weakest, to be treated as *individuals*? Certainly; but that is largely because it has been represented to us that the choice is one of being treated as individuals or not being treated as persons. Our western individualism has made us deeply suspicious of the possibility of human community. We have been told that the great divide is between being treated as individuals and being regimented as part of some collective in which our identity is lost as part of a herd. If the choice is presented that way, the function of pastoral care can only be to offer 'individual attention', and that easily comes to mean the kind of attention which deliberately disregards a person's social location and sees him or her as 'just a human being'. On that basis, spirituality is felt to be merely an aid to the development of that just-a-human-being person which we are supposed to become when our place in the human community is disregarded.

It is true that our social context will not usually be disregarded completely. It is likely, for instance, that our place in our families and in the intimate relationships of our lives will be recognized. Yet what thought has been given to the care, or the prayer, particularly appropriate for a person who is unemployed? or who is engaged in a massive programme of closing down factories? or who is running a rape crisis centre? or who is making bombs? or who is seeking to ban them? What we do know about is a kind of care that is generally applicable to human beings and their life-cycle; it has to do with our loving, our parenting, our dying, our being afraid or sad, well or ill. Being a just-a-human-being kind of person means being one who is engaged in those activities which have to do with the continuing of the human race in much the same way as it has always continued. Our care and our prayer are separated from the tiresome — not to say spiritually demanding — tasks of earning a living, running a country, building a community. They are separated, in short, from all those tasks which belong precisely to the state of being adult, of having to be of age. We do not know what to say about how to pray, how to care and be cared for, in the crucial process of taking adult responsibility for the operation of the human community.

What this amounts to is nothing less than a retreat to biological existence supported by the comfort and collusion not only of religion but also of those agencies — such as medicine or casework — whose profession (what, that is to say, they profess) is caring. What is absolutely clear is that a failure to take responsibility for the operation of the human community and for our place within it does not prevent that community from making crucial decisions. We may have moved away from historic responsibility, that is to say, our responsibility for *how* the human story continues, into biology, being content *that* it continues. But that does not stop historic processes from taking place. The political doctrine that is in the ascendancy in our society at the present time is the fundamentally biological one that, given the minimum of interference, the fittest will be fit; it is a doctrine that accords well with an understanding of pastoral care as attention to individuals just as human beings and of prayer as a species of personal development.

There is no evidence that I am aware of that this official doctrine is in the slightest degree slowing down the process whereby those who do have power within the human community make decisions of historic significance. They decide about weapons, about nuclear-power generation, about employment levels in the industries of the future, about information banks. All these decisions dramatically alter the face of the world and affect our lives and those of future generations. Yet those decisions are frequently taken by people who say at the time that space is being cleared at last for us to make our own decisions, take care of our own selves, live our own lives and generally stop being interfered with.

If one happens to think that most of the historic decisions currently being taken are deplorable, there is still no reason to complain *that* such decisions are being taken. There is no way in which history, the operation of the decisive forces in human society, can be stopped. Work goes on: the world of thinking, speaking, deciding about all those matters which are subject to our capacity to plan and make changes in our lives. We either do our own acting, thinking, feeling — or we get somebody else to do it for us; they either think or decide or act for us, if they are those to whom we have handed over our power of historic decision, or else they become sad, or sick, or imprisoned for us if they are those to whom we have handed over the work of suffering.

There is no doubt, however, that there is something powerfully attractive about the notion that the governing forces in our lives are the forces of nature. It relieves us of the sense of responsibility for those things which we know need changing but which we feel we cannot change. It blames injustice not on decisions made by the powerful but on the natural — and indeed the very valuable — range of individual differences in our makeup and inheritance. It justifies those who do well by claiming that it is nature that has enabled them to do so; it gives to pastoral care the task of enabling people to accept the inevitable.

Yet this is a myth, the myth of origin, the myth that the governing realities of our existence are the ones closest to our animal nature, and it is a cover-up for the fact that we are where we are economically and politically, as powerful or as victims, because human beings have decided that it shall be so. Furthermore this myth, the myth of origin, which is now justifying the loading of ever-increasing suffering on the economically vulnerable, is also the one that serves to justify the exclusion of people from their human inheritance by reason of their race or their sex. For example, even fifty years ago Paul Tillich was able to show what happens to women when the myth of origin becomes the dominant one in society. In words that have a very contemporary ring for us, he

speaks of how the biological function of women in the process
of birth was used by the National Socialists

> to remove women from the public sector — spiritual,
> political and economic — and to put them back into the
> patriarchally structured family, to deprive them of their
> political rights . . .[2]

The operation of this myth enters into and corrupts some of
the central relationship of our lives by declaring that they too
are based on nature and not on historic choices by the human
community. Martin Thornton, the writer on spirituality,
expressed this well in a Sunday colour supplement once
when he voiced, as a country dweller, his irritation at the
description of the beauty of the English countryside as
'natural', when it numbers among its most beautiful features
things like hedges, fields and cottages which are the result of
social history, agricultural development, not to mention sheer
hard work.

It is also untrue that marriage, the family, parenthood are
natural institutions; they are historic in that they are the
product of the work of human societies in making or allowing
to be made decisions about those institutions which will
regulate activities — sex and reproduction, nurture and
rearing — which certainly go on among animals, but which
have not been done 'naturally' since Eden. What happens to
the 'natural' unit of the family and marriage when it is seen
and dealt with as something which is not part of how human
society has organized itself is something I referred to at the
end of Chapter 5.

More alarmingly, we are being told, in the version of the
myth of origin most common at the present time, that the
operation of the economic order is also 'natural', and that the
increasing number of people who have lost their economic
rights through unemployment are doing so because of the
painful, but inexorable, functioning of the laws of economics.
However sad it is, and those who tell us these things are
weeping all the way to the bank, these natural processes have
to be allowed to run their course; indeed, it is the legacy of
attempts by trade unions or socialist or social democratic
governments to interfere with those 'natural' developments
which have made the situation so bad now. Put another way,

the plight of the poor is the result of attempts to bring economics under adult, responsible, historic control in the service of genuine human community. Such attempts to historicize, to bring under the control of people and their intelligence and imagination the working of the economy simply, we are told, make the situation worse.

It was all well said before, by Pope Leo XIII in his encyclical on the Condition of Labour, dated 1891:

> It is impossible to reduce human society to a level. The Socialists may do their worst, but all *striving against nature* is vain. There *naturally* exist among humankind innumerable differences of the most important kind; people differ in *capability,* in *diligence,* in *health* and in *strength*; and unequal fortune is a *necessary* result of inequality of condition. Such inequality is far from being disadvantageous either to individuals or to the community; social and public life can only go on by the help of various kinds of capacity and the playing of many parts, and all persons, as a rule, choose the part which peculiarly suits their case . . . If any there are who pretend differently − and who hold out to a hard-pressed people freedom from pain and trouble, undisturbed repose, and constant enjoyment − they cheat the people and impose upon them, and their lying promises will only make the evil worse than before. There is nothing more useful than to look at the world *as it really is* − and at the same time to look elsewhere for a remedy for its troubles.[3]

Here the myth of origin is clearly stated in words that could figure well in any current manifesto of the political right. The historic forces that have led and continue to lead to inequality are equated with the natural forces that make us all different. To take charge of the human community by a process of historic decision-making is to do violence to the natural differences that characterize the personality of each of us. Looking at the world 'as it really is' is to find it unalterable in the operation of the laws which make society become, by an amazing coincidence, what we find it to be. Evidently looking at the world 'as it really is', that is to say, through the spectacles supplied by the myth of origin, leaves you blind to the insulting absurdity of the claim that 'all persons, as a rule, choose the part which peculiarly suits their case'.

The implications of such a view of the world 'as it really is' for spirituality and pastoral care, are also made abundantly clear. Having looked at the world as it really (that is, naturally and unalterably) is, we shall look 'elsewhere' for a remedy for its troubles. 'Elsewhere', presumably, God will provide a remedy for the shortcomings of a system which is evidently so advantageous; this will not happen by a rectification of the system but by a mixture of grace and philanthropy which will rescue individuals from any disadvantages they may be suffering. We shall assist people to accept the suffering which happens to be their lot in the 'knowledge' that their suffering is the result of a combination of natural forces, a choice they made to be in a particular social situation (even if they cannot remember making that choice) and the wicked machinations and deceptions of socialists doing their worst.

We shall be greatly misleading ourselves if we suppose that what has just been said is a caricature of what pastoral care becomes in the context of a society which has been led to believe that injustice is natural. We shall deceive ourselves even more if we think that our pastoral and spiritual training somehow protects us from such disabling processes. The caring professions are inevitably as locked into what is going on in society at large as ever are trade unionists or boards of directors. We cannot avoid being in the position of ministering to the inner landscape of ourselves and others as it has been shaped by the dominant forces in our society.

It is not that all those engaged in pastoral care have a conscious desire to enable others to conform and to fit in. Nor is it the case that most believers have made some conscious decision to take flight from the world outside into looking after their inner being instead. It is simply that we delude ourselves if we imagine that we can cut ourselves off from social processes as they are currently going on. What we can and must do is to recognize what those social processes are and what, if any, room for manoeuvre they leave us. We also ought to achieve as much clarity as we can about what our aim in pastoral care can be at this present juncture in history and to ensure that our training and our practice assist us in that. That means at least noticing that some very powerful interests are served by the notion that the social order has its roots in biology. For those concerned with the well-being of the human spirit and with the care of persons, to accept that myth would be a retreat indeed. It would be a retreat from the vocation to responsibility which God has given to humankind and into which our history has been propelling us. It would involve surrendering to the desperate idea, which runs quite counter to the dominant strand of the Christian tradition, that our health and salvation and the meaning of our lives can be discerned in separation from the healing and redeeming of the world. To that idea there has to be an alternative.

SEVEN

Taking Sides

However difficult Jill was as a person, I found it appalling when she was evicted from her hostel. Yet when I went to see the warden, it all sounded much more understandable. What seemed to me — with my less demanding and less frequent contact with Jill — to be her admirable independence, was felt by the warden of the hostel to be insufferable stubbornness. Her refusal to accept medical care for her psychological disturbance was not admirable, but on the contrary an intolerable nuisance. The best interests not only of Jill but of everyone else in the hostel would have been served if she had accepted treatment, even if that meant the loss of some of her independence. The only hope was that her eviction might produce that as its result.

It is entirely understandable that the warden of this type of hostel should believe that the residents' best interests are served by the combination of sedation and sentimental religion. The residents are, after all, disturbed and disturbing people; out in the world they cause difficulties for other people and perhaps, as a result, danger to themselves. Yet it happens that such sedation serves other interests too. It serves the interests of the staff who find sedated patients easier to handle; and of a society which finds it preferable that disturbed and disturbing people should be accommodated 'out of the way'. It suits employers, who would rather have employees who work smoothly and cause the minimum of disruption. The way all those interests coincide must raise a question for us. That coincidence of interests is bound to affect the judgement of those whose task it is to care for Jill, even if they believe their task is to look 'solely' after the interests of those in their care.

We live so deeply embedded in that system of interests that it becomes almost impossible for us to see what benefit might ensue from the presence within society, visible and audible, of people who disrupt everything within sight and provoke consequences for themselves which quite properly elicit concern and sympathy from us. How deeply corrupting is that system of interests I do not think we even notice, as we attempt to assess what counsel, or what counselling framework, to offer those who come to us with their disintegrating marriages or their personal difficulties, their raging paranoia or their unconsolable distress. Nor do I think we easily understand how to evaluate that interplay of interests when we examine our own lives and seek for better health, greater singleness of vision, a more balanced lifestyle or a bigger capacity to relax.

I am not suggesting that there is some simple method, some rule of thumb, which can enable us to make the daunting decision to leave ourselves or someone else who may be extremely vulnerable to experience the full force of their own pain or the vengeful attitudes of others. It is no light matter to leave someone to endure further personal deprivation or the coercive power of police or courts. What I observe, however, is that my decisions and my pastoral practice always seem to be pulled in the same direction. The minimizing of pain and the reduction of tension do not appear as one side of an argument, to be balanced against the possible value that disturbance might have. In the end I almost always feel pulled in that direction, and I sense that among pastors I am not alone in that. To notice the way in which our practice seems almost always to take one direction makes clear just how questionable is the offering of pastoral care at all and certainly it raises the question whether seeking a person's individual well-being is always a worthy aim. As we shall see, it puts in a new light some of our most cherished fashions in pastoral methods.

One of the ways in which this one-sidedness shows up is in the vocabulary we have created for ourselves in pastoral care. Attentiveness, empathy, caring, openness, a non-judgemental attitude — these are the virtues in our catalogue of pastoral and spiritual practice. As means to a clearer perception of reality and a greater capacity to act responsibly they are, of course, absolutely vital. They are, however, aims about the immediate situation, about the present. Like many of the goods in a consumer society they are attainable here and now; they create a good experience and a sense of enrichment. It is that immediacy, that possibility of creating out of the counselling relationship something good in itself that makes those virtues so attractive.

This is not to say that the practitioners of either spiritual direction or counselling advertise themselves as offering something instant — many relationships, to be productive, have to be long-term. Very few of those who take pastoral care seriously imagine that answers can be given to serious questions about a person's difficulties in a few sentences in response to a letter. Yet in a society where the attempt to plan our lives together has become deeply suspected and where the greatest good is to possess more, is it possible that the pastor will not be part of that process? The individual concerned and the relationship with the pastor become goals in themselves, and offer the possibility of the realization, without encountering the world outside, of the best possibilities of human existence. The heightening of dissatisfaction, the arousing of a deep longing for the rectification of the social causes of distress — these do not appear very often, in print or in our heads, as goals of the pastoral enterprise.

For those goals to appear, and to appear as important, requires that we should at least consider a new aspect of the pastoral relationship. That aspect involves making pastoral care not only listening but also a taking of sides. It necessitates looking beyond the pastoral relationship itself and beyond the concern with spiritual growth for itself, and asking the questions 'For whom?' and 'For what?' It would involve at the level of fundamental belief having some answer to the question 'What is your hope?' — for yourself and for the person to whom you seek to minister, for those with whom you are in relationship and for the world. It would be a relationship involving the tough demands of discipleship and solidarity, as well as the emotional and intellectual demands of empathy and spiritual openness.

Solidarity is a word much more frequently found in the annals of political struggle and trade-union activity than among the practitioners of pastoral care. Its value is measured not by what it achieves in the present, let alone the satisfaction which it gives to those who are practising it. It is a word forged in struggle, and the need for it arises when the battle lines are drawn. It arises from the recognition that in a disturbed and distorted world loyalties have to be constructed, and that means that solidarity involves not merely the ability to know your friends but also to recognize that there will be those who are opposed to you. Solidarity recognizes that justice and peace in the world are not built up bit by bit through a succession of caring and just relationships but, in a much less tranquil process, by the clash of loyalties in a succession of different but connected struggles. Justice for women and justice for blacks, justice for workers and justice for children, are intertwined issues, held together by the common thread of our search for justice. Yet the process of attaining justice in any one of those areas involves forming loyalties which may separate you from those with whom you have been united in another struggle. Justice itself is an almost indescribable dream, held out as promise in a situation where different hopes and loyalties have to be struggled with. We have to be prepared for defeat as well as victory and we need to be clear which struggle we are waging so that we can be willing if necessary to make new loyalties and surrender old ones.

Pastors speak readily of care, attention and sympathy. Yet if that care, attention and sympathy are needed in a situation characterized by conflict and the unattained longing for justice, the note of solidarity also needs to invade the pastoral relationship. We are not simply concerned with what we attain in the relationship itself at the moment when it is happening. We are also looking for a way to stand alongside one another, and to take one another's side, in the challenge of renewing the face of the earth in justice and peace.

This contrast between care, attention and sympathy as pastors are accustomed to speak of them and the demands of solidarity are best illustrated in relation to a favourite pastoral word: trust. The importance of trust cannot be overestimated, and all who are involved in caring for others take pains to build up that relationship, and know that it takes time. But they generally consider that trust is about creating a relationship of openness in which the truth can be spoken and reality honestly faced. But when those in solidarity with each other speak of trust, they have in mind also something different. They need to ask, in what struggle can I trust you? in what strategies will you stand alongside me? what are the limits to which you will go in this or that cause? Trust is secured in a relationship of solidarity at least as much by being clear what we will not do for someone as it is by being clear what we will. The trust that is created in groups of people can be deeply misleading if these limits of solidarity are not made clear. Time and again we have watched industrial action founder and political campaigns come to grief because warm expressions of support led the campaigners to assume that their supporters would actually stand with them.

We have already seen what our society now expects of pastoral care. It expects care for individuals; it expects that we shall enable them to fit in to what our society demands of them. In such a situation pastors will be reluctant to accept the tough demands of solidarity. It is much easier to say yes and produce a climate of warm support. It is much harder — on ourselves as well as on the people for whom we are caring — to be equally clear about saying no and describing clearly the ways in which we are unwilling to take their side. It is tough on the pastor because it means attaining clarity about the limits of one's own commitment, and that is never easy to face. It is easier to stay within the realm of immediate human relationships that validate themselves here and now; it is easier to leave on one side the unknown outcome of the world's superhuman struggle for justice and peace and instead to settle for the admittedly painful, but at least understandable and manageable quest for human meaning. That those who care about pastoral relationships are reluctant to become engaged on one side of public issues is borne out in my experience of what happens when one discusses political questions with those whose major interest is in pastoral care or spiritual direction.

On the one hand are those who opt for what is the self-styled centre of the political spectrum. There in the centre the irrational extremisms of the right and the left can be forsworn, the danger of lurching from one pole of the ideological spectrum to the other can be avoided and the aims of unity and reconciliation can be pursued with singleminded zeal.

The company is also much more congenial, because on the whole the sort of people who pursue the cause of reconciliation are more congenial people. They are appealing to such worthy objectives as the common good, and it is easy to see why people who are formed by a training in pastoral care, or in spirituality or both, should wish to respond to and pass on such an appeal.

The appeal to the common good is bound, however, to serve whoever happens to have the principal sources of power at their disposal; and even at its face value, the appeal to the common good would depend for its full realization, as Dumas points out, on

> . . . the generosity of the rich, the patience of the poor, the progressive acquisition of private property by the largest possible number, saving them from being exploited and being dependent on the state, and finally on the recognition of God's special concern for the unfortunate and the gift of God's grace in all circumstances to both rich and poor. In short, the common good is an indigestible mixture of courageous and profound spiritual truths with a reverent resignation over natural and social inequalities.[1]

Is it really true, does an honest inspection of the working of the world in which we live, suggest that all conflicts are the result of extreme ideological positions and the warring of interest groups? Is it certain that the way forward to justice for all is a politics that avoids the solidarities and the debates that belong to the struggle for a better world?

The politics of the centre, the politics of the common good, for all their attractiveness contain a real temptation to self-deception. In the process of avoiding, as they think, the partial solidarities of right and left, rich and poor, the politics of reconciliation also support the vested interest of those who support them. The virtues of the political centre are indeed the virtues that have traditionally been fostered in pastoral care, and they are in the interests of those who are, in social terms, in the middle. They do not achieve the reconciliation they seek, and are apt to blame the partisan behaviour of those to right and left of them, without noticing that there is no less partisanship about holding to the middle.

There is, however, an alternative political route which

those pastorally concerned are apt to take. It involves a rather detached attitude to the struggles of the main political parties and institutions and a highly committed stance on those issues which are seen to involve the future of the whole human race. Such issues are peace; conservation of the environment; protection of the earth's non-renewable resources; opposition to nuclear energy. These are felt to be the transcendent issues, the ones that concern all people and not just special interest groups, not even just our own generation but generations to come. They are seen by many of those who campaign about them as the supreme issues of our time. So indeed they are, for they concern the possibility or impossibility of the continued survival of the human race. The campaign for nuclear disarmament and the demand for a lifestyle that does not endanger the limited resources of the earth do not therefore appear as campaigns appealing to our partiality, and we can sense as we participate in them our companionship with the whole human race. They have drawn into them, as campaigns, people who would normally avoid any part in the sectional vested interests of traditional politics. There is no left or right, no rich or poor, no division of classes or races when it comes to peace in the context of weapons of mass destruction or the burial of nuclear waste in our countryside. So the spiritual and pastoral formation of Christians leads them quite naturally into the movement for peace, and for many of us it has been the first major introduction to political activity.

Yet it is an illusion to suppose that it is an introduction to a form of political activity that does not involve partiality, division and conflict, as well as alliance with some interests against others. We may wish to pretend to ourselves that campaigning for peace or for a sustainable lifestyle is something we do for the whole human race, and that we are not 'against' anyone in that process; the reality is quite different. The consumer society, with its inordinate demands on resources, operates in the interests of those who own and hold power in enterprises that profit from the high consumption of resources.

The power of the atom, whether used in weapons of war or to make electricity might (arguably) be operating as a deterrent against our national enemies; it certainly operates

as a deterrent against our own poor. They might otherwise
have nothing to lose by rebellion against those with power in
our society, but the power of the atom offers a pretext for
massive powers of search, arrest, surveillance and control.
Major change in our society involves taking power from those
who have it; and those who have it are now those with their
fingers on the button, who are therefore able to present
themselves as the indispensable protectors of us all.

To be involved in the universal, the global, issues of our
time may look like a way of being political without having
to be involved in the partial solidarities of class or ideology,
and as such may look particularly attractive to those of us
whose concerns are the pastoral, the spiritual and the
individual. They appear more exalted as issues than the very
specific or material concerns of more wages, more jobs,
better houses and schools. But they are not separate issues
and they do not take us out of the realm in which solidarities
have to be chosen and sides taken.

The same is true of those other political issues which seem
at the present time to have a strong claim on those of us
whose formation and whose culture give priority to the
personal, to the world of feelings and inferiority. The politics
of the relation between the sexes, of our treatment of children
and of the old, the issue of homosexual and heterosexual
preference — these issues have a universality about them
that may seem to make them independent of our place in the
economic or social order. I am not suggesting that everyone is
rushing to look those issues in the face; plainly they are not.
Yet for many they have come to assume a centrality that
arises, I suggest, from the fact that they are issues we
somehow *all* face. Like the global questions of the nuclear
debate and of our treatment of the environment, they seem to
be questions everybody can be involved in and everybody has
in some way to face. It puzzles us when those whose causes
are less universal and often more immediately material —
workers' groups, ethnic groups, community organizations —
find preoccupation with a global or personal politics to be a
distraction and a desertion. Their reaction is understandable.
The politics of the universal on the one hand and the intimate
on the other are a spiritualized politics indeed if they are not
linked to the struggles about power and economic well-being

which dominate the lives of the poor and of oppressed groups generally.

What I have said about personal and global politics may seem utterly unacceptable to those involved in these campaigns. Are not the relations of men and women as good an example as any of the unequal distribution of power and money? Is not the issue of peace a clear instance of the way we are trapped by the immense power of a military and economic complex? Is not the treatment meted out to the dissenting minority in matters of sexual preference a matter of coercion? Does not the issue of consumerism, of conservation of non-renewable resources, of personal lifestyle, have its roots in a system of financial rewards which ensures that those who own capital and direct enterprises are bound to put economy before ecology? I would answer all these questions affirmatively. All those issues are crucial. Equally, I am not suggesting, in some punk version of a primitive Marxist economic determinism, that it is the basic relations we have to each other in the economic field which are fundamental, from which all others proceed, and to which we need to give overriding attention.

I am, rather, concerned to make two points. The first is that there seems to me to be some way in which those who have received some pastoral and spiritual formation incline to involvement in some political issues rather than others (if they involve themselves in any). The ones we choose seem to be those which are most clearly universal and which also engage us most at the level of our interior lives. They seem to involve us less in the partial and ambiguous solidarities that most often characterize political activity. My second point is that I suspect that the spiritual and pastoral formation we receive may quite decidedly bias us in that direction. We value the universal and the personal because in our pastoral work we have been encouraged to do so. We wish to be men and women who are building a world of sensitivity and global consciousness and who seek to interact with one another, and particularly, for example, to raise our children with those ideas of sensitivity and global consciousness in their minds. To observe that is not to render the political causes which most embody those ideas unimportant but to present a question to our choice of cause and also raise an issue about the content of our spiritual and pastoral formation.

To personalize the issue, let me refer to the place where I live and work, the conurbation of Tyneside in north-east England. It is a deeply neglected area of the country (not least now) and one which has known the full force of economic hardship. It is lived in by people who have sustained the British economy in good times and bad by the sweat of their brow and the risk, and sometimes the loss, of their lives in coalmines, steel works and shipyards. They have often had to struggle to keep body and soul together in home and community. The depression of the 1930s produced appalling hardship that is etched into the memory of the community, with the Jarrow hunger march as its most powerful symbol.

Partly because of the domination of heavy industry and partly because of the distance of the region from the centre of power in London, economic neglect by politicians and those in charge of industry has ensured a continued climate of economic depression and a problem of unemployment that is endemic. There are families that have known nothing else, and there are schools where more than eighty per cent of those leaving join the ranks of the out-of-work. From such a situation has come a society which is fierce in its loyalty and sense of regional identity, filled with mutual concern in adversity and deeply suspicious of 'them'. A sense prevails that not much can be done about the overarching realities of life, but that in such a context people will do the best they can for each other and defend their way of life. Yet those same conditions are behind some less attractive features of the society. It is frequently brash in its consumerism, when money is there; almost nationally famous in its male domination; quite frequently violent in the raising of children. On issues like the treatment of homosexuals, social attitudes are very rigid indeed.

Where to locate solidarity in that situation? I may have in my mind all sorts of ideas about how the problems of the region are related to national, international and personal issues, but when it comes to the concrete business of political activity there is a dilemma. On the one hand I wish to be associated with the strength of local identity and to support the demand, long overdue and entirely justified, for justice for that community. On the other hand I sense a great distance between my personal values and those of the culture in which I find myself and I am concerned on behalf of the victims of that culture.

My intention here is not to offer some simple, rule-of-thumb answer. I doubt that that is possible, and even if it were, it would hardly be for someone like myself to offer it: I am not the victim of any of the negative cultural traits I have listed. I am concerned to make the point that there is a real conflict and that the way in which I decide my own priorities at any given point is heavily influenced, I notice, by the formation I have received as a Christian and the values that formation has enshrined. I am clear that my pastoral background does bias me, as it does others, to some causes rather than others. However critical those causes may be, however much they may be part of the world's overall struggle for justice, they may not be the ones that are actually clamant for my attention at my present time and place. If that is true, the nature of pastoral training and practice must be due for re-examination. For the criteria for the investment of our energies, and the signs by which we are to identify our vocation at this time and in our particular place need to be strategic ones based on what our strengths are or could be, the ripeness of a particular issue in people's consciousness, the pressing nature of a particular need; the sense that a particular cause might engage me or my friends out of concerns which have been developed in me because of my spiritual or pastoral training needs to be borne in mind with at least a question mark. That is far from easy, because the values we have imbibed in our training to be sensitive and open people are values I have no wish to demean, and the causes to which those values most often draw us are all crucial.

It is interesting to note that this particular dilemma is strongly focused in the book *The Socialist Decision* published by Paul Tillich in Germany in 1933, and already quoted here; the book of which he declared himself to be most proud of any that he had written. It is perhaps significant that, like much material from that decade, the book is arousing renewed attention, and it has been fairly recently reissued in English. Tillich points there to the inherent conflict in the proletarian situation. Workers are by their position, by the exploitation they suffer, uniquely the ones with the power and the need to effect real social change. Yet by virtue of that same position, as dispensable objects in a capitalist society they are likely to be trapped in a range of specific demands that either ignore or actively obstruct the realization of the major hopes of socialist well-being. Only the power, the energy and the specificity of the situation of working people can really achieve change; but those very sources of strength also threaten the genuineness of the political aim. All this, of course, as with much of what I have said, is the kind of thing that can be uttered from a great height by those who have the luxury of making any political choice at all and who are not themselves in the position of being at the bottom of the pile. Yet the spectacle of the Nazi movement, supported as it was by millions of working people, and of many of their successors continuing to support some very reactionary attitudes, means that the dilemma is still a present and serious one.

If what I have said is true about our own pastoral and spiritual formation, we shall be placed in a particular tension about where to locate our solidarity. My concern is that, given the background that we have and the ideals for humanity that we support, we may not even notice that the tension exists. Maybe that goes some way to explaining why there is such a gulf between the Church and working-class people. Church people find the demands made by working people out of their situation unacceptable in the light of their hopes for humanity. The very specific cries of working people, which their situation has called out of them, have hardly been given a chance.

Our difficulty is increased because we make such a highly selective use of our own theological and practical resources. That is true both in our pastoral relationships and in the working out of our own discipleship. We speak as though there were a need to realize, in the here and now, in the counselling situation or the confessional, something complete and whole. We feel required to express then and there those values to which we have chosen to give primacy. Yet we could base our pastoral practice on the great theme of unrealized hope which comes through in the Bible. It speaks of a wholeness and a sensitivity and an openness that are precisely not realizable in the here and now, that belong to a world that is not yet and that are only realizable in the context of the world's struggle for justice and peace.

We choose to create places where we or others can regain our lost wholeness in a life of poise and balance, of spiritual understanding and wisdom. We could be much more eager to challenge those whom we care for to be willing to lose some of the wholeness we have possessed or the poise or spiritual discernment we have achieved in the service of a struggle that has miles to go yet. We leave our praying, people leave our attentive listening, often less prepared than when they came in to offer solidarity to what is less than perfect and to put their effort into a cause that is not all it might be. We need to know that the building of our universal solidarity in the just community of God's good rule is a matter certainly beyond our capacity and almost as far beyond our imagining. The capital of empathy we build up in pastoral encounter needs at some point in the relationship to be opened to the strong wind of challenge. The personal insight needs testing in conjunction with where we and those we care for stand politically.

The desire to realize all there is to be realized here and now and to see the pastoral encounter as an end in itself is simply not what we are here for, and the disciplines of attentiveness we may cultivate are not to dissipate our dissatisfaction and calm our troubled spirits. What we are listening and attending for is ultimately to enable us to invest ourselves more wholeheartedly in the limited visions and specific demands of human beings on the receiving end of society's injustice without forever being afraid of the loss of innocence, wholeness, tranquillity or balance that might ensue. We confess, not in order to re-establish some innocence we fear we may have lost; we are absolved — set free — in order to have precisely the inadequacy and partiality of our own visions made into building blocks out of which the human community is to be made. We are to have a greater readiness to sacrifice most particularly what we see as our virtues in causes whose ambiguity may be all too obvious to us. We are not to listen less or attend less, but to listen and attend to the cry of the world as those whom we care for pastorally express it.

It is the selectivity of our use of our own theological

tradition that conceals from us also the painful fact that often what we see as the best achievements of our pastoral and spiritual traditions can be destructive. When we focus on the God knowable here and now and not on the God of promise and longing, we avoid noticing that we have our own vested interest in a world in which the pastoral virtues flourish. It may indeed be that such a world is a good kind of world; but here and now it is a vested interest of some of us. The quest for that kind of world may indeed not be what most needs to be engaged in at this point. Preparation for the making of strategies, the offering of our solidarity to this cause or that, engagement in conflict and heated argument — these are the demands on our discipleship in a world in which we are 'come of age' in relation to the destiny of the human community, and our care and our prayer need to be appropriate to those who know that the struggle has been committed to us, even as the result of that struggle is ahead and unknown. The spirituality of those who are laying hold of a promise is different and needs to be, from that which belongs to those who imagine that society at large can be disregarded in the interests of creating a good relationship here and now.

If we let ourselves be content with a world fit for the spiritual and pastoral virtues, we are espousing exactly that aspect of liberal theology which Bonhoeffer so accurately criticized. We have already conceded to the world the right to decide on what terms God is to be allowed to continue to rule, and where God's rule can be known — namely, in personal spiritual development and pastoral relationships. We shall have accepted the situation of God at the boundary of human experience, because that is the place where the values in which we have been formed as Christians can still apply.

By contrast, to be involved in the limited solidarities that are part of political activity at the risk of our integrity and of many of the values we may wish to promote is essential for the making of any constructive change in the operation of our corporate situation. In order to be involved in that way we have to recognize that adult responsibility for the situation of humanity in history demands that we join God in the likelihood of God's defeat at the hands of a godless world. As disciples in a world come of age, that is the kind of outcome we should anticipate and see as the fulfilment of the promise which has been set before us. That fulfilment does not come either in the form of a God who will magic the situation right or intervene as an all-powerful tyrant in the end. Nor does it come in the form of a pastoral relationship or spiritual experience which is so satisfying in itself that it becomes all we seek and our longing is satisfied.

Pastoral practice has to be politically and socially aware. Spiritual discipline has to locate us somewhere in the world's struggle. That has become clear in our exploration. It means not less listening and attentiveness but a determination to lead relationships to the point where they are located politically and where they lead to facing people's full situation; and that means their situation in the network of oppression, liberation, injustice and justice which are features of our lives together. Philip has to be listened to to find where his remoteness from issues outside his own life can be challenged. It is an act of pastoral care to invite the hostel warden to consider again whether the sedated residents might not have some better way of channelling their discontent. The biblical stories of healing and teaching need to be read, by those whose ministry is to heal the minds and spirits of people, as being forged in the harsh world of conflict when they were written and as having something to say to such a world now. So it turns out, not at all surprisingly, that the need to look at context when we are engaged in pastoral care stems from what is basically a theological claim. If we are going to pray, and if we are going to care for others, it will demand of us the most radical understanding of what our religious tradition actually offers to the world.

On the one hand we pray and we care, not in any world we happen to make for ourselves, a private world or a world shared with a few friends; we pray and we care in this world, a real world whose disturbance and social dislocations have their reflection in the disturbance and dislocation of people as they engage in the quest for meaning in their lives, a meaning above and beyond mere survival. That disturbance and dislocation in the world are frequently related to the disturbance of individuals and have their manifestation in phenomena as varied as physical sickness, a crisis in relationships or a sense of meaninglessness and despair. The superhuman struggle of the world for the realization of justice and peace invades the search of human beings for meaning in their lives. It is the privilege of pastors to hear that world speak in the voices of those individuals to whom they listen. Their faith and their practice are to be radicalized by what they hear.

On the other hand, for those whose care and whose prayer claim to be Christian, there is another context. It is provided by the story they tell and the proclamation they make about the One to whom they pray and for and with whom they do their caring for each other. That the life of the world should as a matter of experience invade the counselling session, the prayer time and our every attempt at growing in spiritual discernment is precisely what is to be expected if the world is indeed loved and sustained in life by that God of whom Christians speak. For that God is claimed to be committed through thick and thin and at whatever cost not to situations which happen to be suitable for good relationships or to people who happen to have leisure or aptitude for attentiveness or for growing spiritually, but on the contrary to situations where relations are distorted and where structures oppress. If there is weeping in heaven at cities which do not know what belongs to their peace then it would be surprising if there could be places where human meaning could be found without the tears and the anger of the world invading.

The historic context of pastoral care turns out also to be its theological context; its place in the history of the struggle of humanity for the discovery of a wholesome life together turns out also to be its place in the story of God's own struggle that none of us, no situation of distress or frustration, oppression or exploitation should remain unredeemed. It is always uncertain whether that history of the world and of God will have a future, whether there is anything on ahead worth striving for either for those individuals whose lives are distorted in any number of ways or for the scarred and divided common life of humanity. It is always possible, and it will always happen, that for some that question will have to have a negative answer: there is no future; or there is no God; or there is no meaning. What is clearly intolerable is that those who claim to be believers should say that they are giving an affirmative answer to the question of God while at the same time they implicitly deny that there is anything worth struggling after in the common life of humanity. They cannot be content to offer meaning to individuals while consigning their context to effective oblivion. For what believers claim is the context of the whole of life, private and public, is the unremitting faithfulness that lies at the heart of everything. That faithfulness grieves over the sufferings and rages over the injustices of people, and at the same time deems the promise that is hidden in human history worth the risk of ultimate failure, defeat at the hands of a godless world.

It is because of the nature of that context that the spiritual tradition of Christianity has the form it has. The material legacy of that tradition is not a manual of discipline; the legacy is essentially the solidarity of those who have struggled before us. We have prophets who were inspired to prophesy and wished the inspiration would go away. We have psalms of celebration and lament. We have saints with triumphant proclamations to make and others who are remembered for denial and doubt. And we claim to be led by one whose ministry is remembered for unfailing obedience to a task laid upon him, a longing that that task might be taken away and a sense of ultimate aloneness in the midst of it all. Yet this tradition does not offer itself as a ragbag of individual experience but as the way in which God's struggle through success and failure for a purpose worth everything was reflected in the uncomfortable lives of God's followers. There were many times when the longing of those followers for some sense of meaning, apart from the divine purpose for the world, came to expression — and there were many times when that longing was refused.

One characteristic feature of that tradition is the constant offering, rejection and enlargement of humanity's responsibility for the world it inhabits. Our forebears were offered responsibility for the destiny of Israel and asked for a king to take the responsibility for them. The divine response, in Jesus of Nazareth, was a handing back of the responsibility, not this time for Israel only but for humanity even to the ends of the earth. We have invented hierarchies of Church and State to take that responsibility off our shoulders. Yet they fail, or turn to oppression, and in their failure we have constantly been invited into more and more accountability with fewer and fewer excuses. Time and again there has come to expression, both religiously and politically, a deep desire for someone somewhere to lift the burden from our shoulders, and our every attempt to call in aid some mechanism, some person, some skill has rebounded on us as we have found ourselves with yet another thing to be responsible for, and the one voice we hear again and again through the events of our history seems to say 'Take charge'.

It is one of the great opportunities of the pastoral vocation as I have endeavoured to describe it, to mediate that call as well as to hear it. In the developing understanding we have gained about pastoral care, and particularly the importance of listening and attentiveness, we have borne witness to the fact that the taking charge is not to be a species of domination or loading other people with our answers. We have frequently encountered unbelievable reserves of affection and co-operation in helper and helped, and often experienced an amazing journey into mutuality and friendship.

What we can now see is that the taking charge is limitless in its scope but nonetheless fraught with risk. Not only might we fail in our attempt to take charge, and that could be bad enough. We might have to enter into processes, of politics or conflict, that are a far cry from where we should like to be. We might have to leave behind and not rest in the modes of humanity and compassion that we can, often at least, realize in pastoral relationships. The risk is that we might forsake, or encourage others to forsake, the hardwon inner fulfilment which was what we thought pastoral care had to offer to people. Furthermore, we might forsake that fulfilment for something as uncertain in its outcome as the movement towards a just and peaceful earth.

A range of issues have come to the surface in our exploration of pastoral care, some of them momentous. What is just as important is that a number of individuals have borne us company in the exploration, individuals who have sat with me and shared the inner drama of their lives. These have been actual men and women all of whom have brought to the surface, without intending to, fundamental questions about the place of pastoral care in our public struggles.

The first image returns. In the child's total absorption in

his falling, failure, tears and frustration, there is no sign that he even entertains any hope of getting to his feet again. The child walking erect across the room seems not to entertain any thought of failure. We seem to be asked, in the service of our responsibility for the full range of issues that are within our grasp at this point in history, to ally ourselves strongly where the need is and to experience also the collapses and the drastic reappraisals that follow them. To become again people who can do that seems to be a kind of spirituality to which our tradition points, as it witnesses to victories and defeats both of which appear to be presented as total. The full significance of our search for meaning is that it always exemplifies some part of the world's struggle for justice and peace, and the meaning our lives can have is that we are responsible participants in that struggle, prepared to stand and to fall, for the sake of the promise that is set before us.

Notes

Chapter 2

1. See his *The Moral Context of Pastoral Care.* Westminster Press 1976.
2. See his *The Dynamics of Religion: Process and Movement in Christian Churches.* Darton, Longman & Todd 1978.
3. N. Kazantzakis, *The Saviors of God* (Simon & Schuster 1960), p. 55.

Chapter 3

1. See E. Bethge, *Dietrich Bonhoeffer — a Biography.* Collins 1970.
2. *Letters and Papers from Prison,* ed. E. Bethge (SCM Press 1971), pp. 325-6.
3. Ibid., p. 326.
4. Ibid., p. 327.
5. *Markings* (Faber 1966), p. 74.

Chapter 4

1. Lao-tze, in C. Rogers, *A Way of Being* (Houghton Mifflin 1980), p. 42.
2. Rinehart, *The Book of EST* (Holt, Rinehart & Winston 1976), p. 22.
3. C. Rogers, op. cit., p. 115.
4. *The Politics of Experience* and *Bird of Paradise* (Penguin 1970), p. 12.

Chapter 5

1. K. Gibran, *The Prophet* (Heinemann 1972), p. 49.
2. Ibid., pp. 50-1.
3. D. Bonhoeffer, op. cit., p. 360.
4. See L. Blue, *To Heaven with Scribes and Pharisees, The Lord of Hosts in Suburbia, The Jewish Path to God* (Darton, Longman & Todd 1975), p. 22.

5. D. Bonhoeffer, op. cit., pp. 348-9.
6. See W. R. Bion, *Experiences in Groups and Other Papers.* Tavistock Publications 1968.

Chapter 6

1. K. Gibran, op. cit., p. 91.
2. P. Tillich, *The Socialist Decision* (Harper & Row 1976), p. 31 — Eng. tr.
3. A. Dumas, *Political Theology and the Life of the Church* (SCM Press 1978), p. 121.

Chapter 7

1. A. Dumas, op. cit., p. 121.

Further reading

Bion, W. R., *Experience in Groups, and Other Papers.* Tavistock Publications 1968.

Blue, L., *To Heaven with Scribes and Pharisees.* Darton, Longman & Todd 1975.

Browning, D., *The Moral Context of Pastoral Care.* Westminster Press 1976.

Coles, R., *Children of Crisis: A Study of Courage and Fear.* Faber & Faber 1968.

Edwards, T., *Spiritual Friend.* Paulist Press 1980.

Ellul, J., *Prayer and Modern Man.* Seabury Press 1970.

Fairbairn, A., *Five Smooth Stones.* Bantam Books 1969.

Fromm, E., *Fear of Freedom.* Routledge & Kegan Paul 1942.

Hammarskjöld, D., *Markings.* Faber & Faber 1964.

Heyward, I. C., *The Redemption of God.* University Press of America 1982.

James, M., and Jongeward, D., *Born to Win: Transactional Analysis with Gestalt Experiments.* Signet Books 1978.

Kazantzakis, N., *The Rock Garden.* Simon & Schuster 1963.

Kazantzakis, N., *The Saviors of God.* Simon & Schuster 1963.

Kesey, K., *One Flew Over the Cuckoo's Nest.* Pan Books 1973.

Kook, Abraham Isaac, *The Lights of Penitence, Lights of Holiness, Moral Principles, Essays, Letters and Poems.* SPCK 1979.

Laing, R. D., *Politics of Experience* and *Bird of Paradise.* Penguin 1970.

Lambourne, R. A., *Community Church and Healing.* Darton, Longman & Todd 1963.

Leech, K., *Soul Friend.* Sheldon Press 1977.

Leech, K., *Youthquake.* Sheldon Press 1973.

Moltmann, J., *The Crucified God.* SCM Press 1976.

Moltmann, J., *The Future of Creation.* SCM Press 1979.

Niebuhr, R., *Man's Nature and His Communities.* Scribner 1967.

Passons, W. R., *Gestalt Approaches in Counselling.* Holt, Rinehart & Winston 1975.

Perls, F., *The Gestalt Approach and Eye Witness to Therapy.* Bantam Books 1976.

Roszak, T., *Where the Wasteland Ends: Politics and Transcendence in Post-industrial Society.* Faber & Faber 1974.

Selby, P., *Look for the Living.* SCM Press 1976.

Thornton, E. E., *Theology and Pastoral Counselling.* Fortress Press 1964.

Williams, R., *Resurrection.* Darton, Longman & Todd 1982.

Index